"Love you,
Daddy Boy"

"*Love you,*

DAUGHTERS HONOR THE

TAYLOR TRADE PUBLISHING

Daddy Boy"

FATHERS THEY LOVE

Edited by Karyn McLaughlin Frist

LANHAM • NEW YORK • BOULDER • TORONTO • OXFORD

Published by Taylor Trade Publishing
An imprint of The Rowman & Littlefield Publishing Group, Inc.
4501 Forbes Boulevard, Suite 200, Lanham, Maryland 20706

Distributed by NATIONAL BOOK NETWORK

Library of Congress Cataloging-in-Publication Data
"Love you, daddy boy" : daughters honor the fathers they love / [edited by] Karyn McLaughlin Frist. — 1st Taylor Trade pub. ed.
        p. cm.
   ISBN-13: 978-1-58979-368-2 (cloth : alk. paper)
   ISBN-10: 1-58979-368-4 (cloth : alk. paper)
 1. Fathers and daughters. I. Frist, Karyn McLaughlin, 1954-
   HQ755.86.L68 2006
   306.874'2—dc22   2006009778

∞ The paper used in this publication meets the minimum requirements of American National Standard for Information Sciences—Permanence of Paper for Printed Library Materials, ANSI/NISO Z39.48-1992.

Manufactured in the United States of America

To my father, Bill Edd McLaughlin , whose memory will always be with me, and to the love of his life, my mother, Kathryn Loving McLaughlin, whose support and love I will always feel.

To my husband, Bill, whose support and moral compass has been an example of how to live life for our sons, Harrison, Jonathan, and Bryan, whom I hope some day will be blessed by knowing the joy of being fathers.

Contents

Introduction

■ Karyn McLaughlin Frist

ON EASTER SUNDAY, 2002, I dedicated an outdoor garden chapel that I designed for Daddy. It has a bronze plaque that says:

> This outdoor chapel
> is dedicated in memory of
> William E. McLaughlin II
> 1923–1982
> Ephesians 6:1–3 ". . . honor your father
> and mother."
> Easter 2002

This book honors fathers around the world. From the countryside of Romania to the fashion industry of New York and Italy or the farm fields in rural Tennessee, fathers are instrumental in the shaping of our morals and values.

"Not a day goes by that I don't think of my dad." Over the past two years that I have been working on this book, I have heard those words many times. Women's voices would rise two octaves as they started talking about their fathers. Justice Sandra Day O'Connor's voice, low at first when I called her in her Supreme Court chamber about my project, rose and softened when I explained that I was gathering stories about fathers. My short conversations with women often turned into an hour call. We ended with them saying, "I can think of so many things to write. Thank you for asking me."

My inspiration for this book came during a National Prayer Breakfast, an event at which President Bush was introducing then National Security Advisor Condoleezza Rice. I had always admired Condi's stature, intelligence, and poise. At the end of the introduction, the president said, "Condi, your father would be proud of you." At that moment, this stoic woman could barely contain her emotion. I instantly thought of my dad and felt the same way. Later that month I observed Jenna Bush at the White House arriving late to a small dinner for the King of Spain. Her father, President George W. Bush, at first seemingly annoyed that she was late, took one look at Jenna as she hurriedly slipped into the room, and absolutely melted. He broke into a big, proud smile, and we all sat down for dinner.

I thought all that night about the unique, special relationship between daughters and fathers—tortience, as contributor Mary Higgins Clark notes, is what they call this bond on Cape Cod. It's pervasive.

Senator Kay Bailey Hutchison noted, "I have always wanted to mention my dad when I speak, but I get choked up and have never been able to. Now I can."

As word about this book spread, I had women come up to me and say, "My dad was great," and proceed to tell me wonderful and inspiring stories about their dads. I am just sorry that I could not include every story in this book.

This project has grown from a small idea to a wonderful gift—not only to the women and fathers who have contributed, but also to anyone who has shared this special relationship with their father. No matter what socioeconomic background, country, or profession the contributors have come from, the undercurrent remains a steadfast love of their dads.

First ladies, U.S. senators, a governor, Hollywood actresses, Grand 'Ole Opry artists, Olympic gold medalists, the most winning women's basketball coach in the country, and an American soldier describe the foundation their fathers gave them to dream and reach for the highest star—often overcoming great obstacles and surviving because of their fathers' love and unwavering support for them.

Women from five countries and more than twenty states have opened their hearts to give us a peek into their lives with their fathers. Daughters of a U.S. president, a Holocaust survivor, baseball Hall of Fame legends, a NASCAR driver, a New York fashion designer, and a hero from 9/11 share lessons learned—not always easy—and tender moments with their fathers.

The first woman president of an African country, the first woman president of Princeton University, the first Mexican American woman to enter the male-dominated world of golf, the first woman to preside over the highest court in our country, and a daughter of a civil rights leader all reflect on the guidance their fathers had in shaping their lives and encouraging them when life was not always easy.

As I assembled the various stories from across the world, I tried to think of a title that would encompass the feeling of the final piece. I saved many letters that my dad wrote me when I was in college. Daddy wrote me every Monday and signed his letters "Love you, Daddy Boy." I will never forget his letters and his love for me. This book is a chance for me, as well as for every woman, to say "I love YOU, Daddy Boy" to their fathers.

I am so honored and inspired by these great women and their stories. I hope you will be as well. If you are so moved, write about your own father in the space provided at the end of the book. Wherever he might be, I'm sure he would smile if you did so.

Many of the wonderful fathers you will read about are no longer with us. Indeed, some have passed away in the brief time that this book was written. I hope these essays will serve as a meaningful and lasting tribute. And I'm sure I speak for all of these women when I say enjoy every day with your father and family. Treasure every precious moment.

"Love you,
Daddy Boy"

Stefanie Honoré-Acosta
Kimberly Honoré

■ Russel L. Honoré

EVEN BEFORE our father became widely recognized during the aftereffects of Hurricane Katrina, anyone who knew him or worked with him throughout the years always seemed interested in knowing what he was like as a father. Recognized for his direct approach and strong personality, he is known to many in the military as the "Ragin' Cajun," and we can honestly say that this name fits him perfectly.

There was many a Saturday morning when he seemed to resemble "The Great Santini" a little too much by waking us up at a ridiculously early time when the whole of humanity was still sleeping. He pulled at our feet and at an insanely loud octave screamed, "Rise and shine," in which case we are pretty sure he was able to wake up anyone within a five-mile radius.

Grudgingly we got out of our beds, dressed, ate a quick breakfast (referred to as chow by our dad), and by 7 a.m. we were out in the yard ready to seek and destroy our assigned chores. Washing cars, cutting grass, weeding flower beds, bathing the dog—It seemed our father was a cruel taskmaster. We mumbled to each other that if we had a "normal" father we'd be laying on the sofa watching Saturday morning cartoons while eating a nice sugary bowl of cereal. Instead we were out cutting the grass for the second time in a week because we happened to have a dad who majored in agriculture and didn't believe in cutting the grass "too short."

Our father was also notorious for giving out nicknames to everyone he ever met. It was rare to hear him ever call us by our given names. Instead of Stefanie, Michael, Kimberly, and Steven, we were referred to as Peaches, Cooter Brown, Weasey, and Baby Brother. Most people would find this en-

dearing; however, their parents, who probably also had nicknames for them, refered to them by their given names when they had friends over. Our father not only called us by our nicknames, but he also issued nicknames to all of our friends. During your teenage years when everything about your parents seems to embarrass you, this was probably the most mortifying of our dad's habits.

And just in case you're wondering, yes—we did have to hear all of his famous one-liners, such as "don't get stuck on stupid," on a daily basis. We always joke that he should write country-western songs when he retires. But as much as we tease him, we find ourselves using many of the same one-liners.

As quirky and strict as our father was during our formative years, growing up with him as our anchor was a lot of fun; although he is strict, he is also kind, warm, and overtly hilarious. He is a very generous man, and we are not just referring to all of the material things that a parent can give to you. Our father is generous with his heart—always making time for us when we need him most.

To this day, any time we need to speak to him, he is always available to us. In fact, there has always been a standing order for all of his staff: if his wife or children call for him, it doesn't matter if he is meeting with the president of the United States, we are to be put through immediately. This proved to be true during the days following Hurricane Katrina, when one of us called and he was indeed in a meeting with the president. It took some serious negotiation skills to convince his aide de camp that it would not get back to our dad that one of us had called. Let's face it—who wants to be the child who interrupts the president?

Everything our father has done has always been for his family; any sacrifice that he needed to make in order to assure that we had what we needed was done with no regret. Because of his selflessness and devotion to us, we can honestly say that we have all turned out to be strong individuals and successful adults.

People always tell our parents how impressed they are to see that they have raised two daughters who are confident and successful at what they do. We have never depended on anyone to make things happen for us, and we don't sit around all day wondering why we can't have Cindy Crawford's legs like a lot of other women do. Our father raised us to realize that, although looks fade, brains last forever. For the two of us the confidence that he instilled in us and the love that he continuously provided us has proved to be the greatest gift he has ever given us. Our father has always been, and will always be, our hero.

■ ■ ■

Stefanie Honoré-Acosta, 34, lives in St. Petersburg, Florida, with her husband, James, and son, James Russel; she is the director of administration for a local electronic retailer. *Kimberly Honoré*, 24, relocated to St. Petersburg, Florida, leaving New Orleans after Hurricane Katrina. Kimberly is a PR/marketing director for a local electronic retailer.

Lieutenant General *Russel L. Honoré*, recently Commander of Joint Task Force Katrina, commands the First United States Army in Atlanta, Georgia, responsible for the training and readiness of National Guard and Reserve forces throughout the continental United States; he has served in various command and staff positions during his 35-year career, ranging from the Middle East and Korea, to Europe and Washington, DC.

Kelly Garcia Arrillaga

■ ANDY GARCIA

THE TOWHEADED little girl turned wide-eyed to her dad, who was in the driver's seat. "Are we almost there?" she asked. "Yes, almost there," her dad answered. The yellow Volkswagen square-back bumped along the road, cheerfully taking all the turns and vibrating as if it were just as excited as the child to get to their destination. She turned ahead, hands on the edge of her seat in anticipation of their arrival.

As the car sputtered to a stop, her dad reached up to the hand crank to open the sunroof. "One, two, three, four," the little girl counted out loud the turns of the handle. Once the sunroof was open, he carefully lifted his daughter up so that she could sit on the roof with her legs dangling inside the car. Ponytails flying in the wind, she clapped her hands. "What's that one? What's that one?" she cried as the thunderous sound passed over the car. "That's a Boeing 727. See how it has an engine on each side and one on the top," he pointed out to her. "Ohhhhhh, yes! I see them!" A few seconds later she excitedly pointed, "Look at the one with the smiley face! What is that one? That one has three engines too!" "That's an L-1011, Kelly," he answered. He smiled at his little girl, legs swinging back and forth inside the car, eyes up to the sky, waiting for the next plane.

I think I could identify different aircraft just by the sounds of their engines by the age of six or seven. Since that very first clear memory of sitting on the sunroof with my dad at the airport, I decided that I wanted to fly. As I got older, the dream of someday piloting my own plane didn't fade. My dad and I continued to go to air shows and we watched WINGS (not the sitcom but the documentary show) on the history channel. Each week a different aircraft was featured, and we couldn't wait to learn all about it. When I wrote the essay for my college applications, I wrote a story about owning my own charter seaplane business on a tropical island.

What I now realize is that time with my dad was never just about the planes. Quality time was a priority for him, and it was always special for me. It was not only a time of fun and sharing a love of aviation, but a time when I learned about looking at the world through the eyes of a dreamer and having the confidence to achieve those dreams. My dad made me feel that anything was possible as long as I put my mind to it.

As much as my dad encouraged me to believe in my dreams and gave me confidence to believe in myself, he gave me the freedom to accomplish those dreams by myself. I don't think I appreciated it at the time, but standing back and allowing me to achieve my dreams on my own was just as important as instilling in me the ability to dream.

When I was in college, I finally made up my mind to learn how to fly. I got a job at Cinema Air Jet Center, an FBO at the Palomar Airport north of San Diego, and made friends with the flight instructors in the neighboring hangar. I was a student at UC San Diego and began taking lessons in between classes and work. My dad was supportive and continued to offer encouragement, but reminded me that school was my first priority. I remember actually wanting more help with the flying lessons at the time. He must have known that, if this dream was that important to me, then I would find a way to make it happen. After nine months I earned enough hours to be eligible to take both the practical and written exams, and I passed both. I achieved my very first dream!

Now, thirty years later, I still run outside and look up at the sky through the eyes of that four-year-old little girl whenever I hear certain aircraft flying overhead. I can't help but smile, and thank my dad.

■ ■ ■

Kelly Garcia Arrillaga grew up in Portola Valley, California, and graduated from the University of California, San Diego, with a degree in creative writing. She is a Certified Trust and Financial Advisor and works as a trust officer at a large financial institution. She lives in the San Francisco Bay Area with her husband and son.

Andy Garcia was born and raised in Sunnyvale, California, and graduated from San Jose State with a degree in business. He was the co-founder and president of Cinco Group, Inc., a successful industrial equipment company. Andy was a devoted husband, father, son, and brother and was one of the forty heroes aboard United Flight 93 who gave their lives for our freedom in the first war against terror.

Maria Ignez Barbosa

■ SERGIO CORRÊA DA COSTA

THE INVITATION to write about my father came less than a month after his death. I was still trying to overcome the disappearance of someone who was lucid, enjoying life, writing books, and remaining generous to his family and friends.

At the age of eighty-six, after a long and successful career devoted to his country, having served as ambassador to London, the United Nations, and Washington, he was still handsome, elegant, and wore the same size as he did in his youth.

Although I was well aware of my father's ability to make things happen, and grew up surrounded by his extreme efficiency, I was surprised to receive letters, notes, e-mails, or unexpected calls from people telling me some story about how a small gesture or act of generosity of his had made a difference in their lives or even changed some of their destinies.

An example is the story of Julio Matteus, a Brazilian who lives in Dallas, where he owns a chain of steak houses. Aged nineteen, dreaming of going to America and having been refused a U.S. visa three times in Brazil, he decided to go to London as an exchange student in the hope of obtaining a U.S. visa there. Crying in the rain after waiting in line for several hours at the U.S. Consulate only to be turned down again, suddenly he thought of the Brazilian Embassy. Twelve blocks later he arrived, soaking wet, begging to talk to the ambassador. By chance, my father overheard the secretary asking the boy if he had an appointment and asked her to send him in. He realized that the boy was well intentioned and had enough money to travel, so he picked up the phone and called the U.S. Consul General, who knew that my parents were close friends of the U.S. Ambassador Walter Annenberg and his wife Lee. It was only in 2003 that Matteus managed to discover the name and address of my father who then learned of his success in life, and of his gratitude.

My father's capacity to deliver whatever was expected from him was well known in our Ministry of Foreign Affairs. When he became Deputy Foreign Minister, an old ambassador under whom he had served took the microphone to say that every time he asked my father to do something he could go to bed without worry: "There was no risk, the following day, of hearing from Sergio that the telex didn't work, that the person in charge was on vacation, or that the mission was not accomplished because it was a holiday in country X. He would always figure out a way, and never came back with an excuse."

One story that may be amusing now, but was not so much then, is that of when he was asked by the Foreign Minister of Brazil to look after Eva Peron when she attended the first pan-American conference after WWII, held at the famous Quitandinha Hotel in Petrópolis, near Rio, in August of 1947. Secretary of State George Marshall was representing President Truman who, to show the importance of the event, went to the airport to say goodbye to his envoy. Argentina had been pro-Axis during the war and Evita had decided to show up, uninvited. My father's mission was to find a way to keep her from addressing the conference, and he did so by taking her to the wrong conference rooms and confusing her with the timetable.

When my husband was posted as ambassador to London in 1993, some twenty or so years after my father, we were so thrilled at the prospect of living in the same house where my parents had lived that I sent him a fax announcing the news in just one line: God save the Queen. With the sense of humor that never abandoned him, he wrote back offering my husband his top hat: "He just needs to carry it on his hand; it's not important if it fits his head. Has he got a black overcoat? If it's grey, blue, or has little squares, it will not be tolerated." To really scare us he went on to tell the obviously invented story of an ambassador whose credentials were refused because of a grey overcoat. "The poor guy withdrew to Tokyo and, word has it, committed hara-kiri. In short, London is a post where you have to take futility seriously."

In 1999, when we were sent to Washington, maybe the most important and demanding post of our career, again in his footsteps, I am sure that the fact that he had been there before made me feel immediately at ease in our new job.

Although he teased me, saying that I didn't have much of a sense of humor, he used to say that we had both inherited the talent to write from his grandfather, a well-known Brazilian poet. I remember how proud he was of my articles during my early years as a journalist in Rio de Janeiro. In 1968, before I got married, my father and I had a joint book launching party at the Copacabana Palace Hotel. His book was *The Four Crowns of Peter I*, while mine was a collection of interviews with well-known Brazilians and others like Salvador Dali and Tom Stoppard.

One of my favorites among his books—he was a member of the Brazilian Academy of Letters—is one first published in French, called *Mots sans Frontières*. It won two important literature prizes in France, and catalogues words from different languages that have migrated to others and are recognizable everywhere, like striptease, voyeurism, and coup de foudre, a subject that had always interested him. Many years earlier, on meeting John Glenn, the famous astronaut, he asked him, "Why is it that when you talk about spacecrafts meeting each other you always use the word rendezvous?" The answer was that neither the Americans nor the Russians had found a better equivalent. The French were, of course, thrilled that the book concludes that, in spite of the increasing advances of the English language, French was still the origin of the greatest number of expressions that have turned global.

In the void opened after his death, I often find myself laughing at the memory of his very special and witty phrases, feeling his supporting presence, and, most of all, continuing to learn from his legacy and example.

■ ■ ■

Former Brazilian Ambassadress to London and the United States, journalist, and interior designer, Maria Ignez Barbosa currently lives in Sao Paulo, Brazil.

Ambassador Sergio Corrêa da Costa was one of the most respected diplomats in Brazil and served as ambassador to the UK, the UN, and Washington, DC during the seventies and eighties. A historian and member of the Brazilian Academy of Letters, he authored many books on Brazilian history and diplomacy.

Mary Frist Barfield

■ THOMAS F. FRIST, SR.

O NE SUNDAY several years ago, Lloyd Ogilvie, a distinguished
Presbyterian minister and former chaplain of the United States Senate, preached a sermon on "being blessed to be a blessing." God often blesses one to touch the lives of others. I left the sanctuary thinking of my
father and of the blessing he had been to me and to all who knew him.

One of my earliest memories of Dad is an Easter weekend when I was
only five years old. I joined him on a special train trip from our home in
Nashville to visit his elderly mother in Florida. I shall never forget sharing
this special time with him. Dad loved his mother dearly as she had reared her
four children after the tragic and untimely death of his father, who died from
injuries suffered in saving the life of a woman and her young grandchild.
Throughout his life Dad spoke of his devotion to his mother and of the influence she had in shaping his character. In the same way, he made an impact on
the lives of others.

Dad was tall with red hair, a warm smile, and a twinkle in his eye. He
lived a life of compassion, enthusiasm, and strong moral character. He was a
caring physician, beloved by his patients for his gentleness, for his genuine
concern for them, and for making time to listen. They revered him for his
positive words of wisdom and for offering hope and encouragement. To this
day I often meet former patients and their families who share wonderful and
heartwarming stories of Dad's devotion to them as their physician and friend.

When I was growing up our family home was always busy with five children, three boys and two girls, a menagerie of animals, a large barn, and a host
of neighborhood friends enjoying the warm and fun-filled atmosphere that
my parents provided. Dad was a wonderful father. He loved, praised, and encouraged us. He was a man of integrity, humility, and faith, who taught us the
importance of being thankful for our blessings and of showing kindness to

others. Each night after seeing patients all day, Dad came home for dinner and devoted this time entirely to the children. He captivated us in engaging conversation, competitive games, and suspenseful bedtime stories. He said our prayers with us and often teased us if we were not kneeling at the bedside: "God may not hear a lazy man's prayers." When all was settled, he returned to the hospital to complete patient rounds or he made house calls, often taking one of us with him. We were proud of him as a loving and attentive father and as one who also cared for others.

From the time I was young, I felt a special bond with my father. I was his youngest daughter and was often found close by his side. He shared my love for horses and playing outdoor games with my siblings and friends. As I grew up he encouraged, inspired, and supported me. I listened and learned from him. I loved Dad for his enthusiasm for life and for those around him. He always looked for the good in other people and had a gift for bringing out their best. Because of his confidence in me, I wanted to live up to his expectations and never disappoint him. He would often say: "Good people beget good people," encouraging us to surround ourselves with persons of good moral character. By his example he taught us that it was important to try to leave the world a better place.

Dad was devoted to my mother and often praised her for "being the most wonderful wife a man could ever have." She was a remarkable person, reaching out to others in need while being a mother whose energy, love, and support were boundless. Dad's love and respect for her influenced my view that being a good wife and mother were the most important roles for me in my own life. My dad believed that a strong family, a vital spiritual life, and a commitment to serving others were the foundation for a life of happiness and fulfillment.

In January of 1998, Dad passed away and Mother died soon after she learned he was gone. The eulogy given at their joint funeral by a family friend and physician partner of my father described their lives so beautifully: "One death is the end of a long and illustrious life. Two deaths is a love story." Their fourteen grandchildren, who were devoted to them, carried the caskets from the sanctuary. The memory of my father is always with me and the legacy of his life is a blessing to all who know his story.

•••

Mary Frist Barfield is one of Dr. Frist's five children and lives in Nashville, Tennessee, with her husband, four children, and five grandchildren.

Dr. *Thomas F. Frist, Sr.*, was a physician, founder of HCA, Inc., formerly known as Hospital Corporation of America, Inc., husband and father of five children, including U.S. Senate Majority Leader Bill Frist of Tennessee.

Cathleen Black

■ JIM BLACK

WHEN I THINK about my father, Jim Black, the first thing that pops into my head is a bigger than life man. He was tall and handsome and dynamic. When he walked into a room, he had that gift of "presence." He was strong and charismatic and people were naturally drawn to him. When I was little, I used to love to sit with him on our front porch and just chatter away, filling him in on my various daily activities. I really loved going to his office on Saturdays, where my favorite place was the stockroom. Of course, I would come home with my pockets laden with notepads and pencils and erasers. It was better than shopping at Marshall Field and Company, our local department store in Chicago, my hometown.

A great tragedy happened to our family when my dad was 52. He lost his eyesight and was blind for 11 years before his death at 63 of a heart attack. I was about 16 when his eyesight started failing, and, by the time I went to college, he was totally blind. With something like this comes anger, frustration, heartbreak, hope, and denial. When I went away to college, probably the greatest gift my folks could have given me considering the circumstances, I never even told my roommate that my dad was sightless. I suppose I wanted to be just like everyone else. Dad talked about his frustration of having to learn how to do things that were once the simplest of tasks or the realization that there were some things he just would never be able to do. Unfortunately, my father never regained his sight, in spite of the best efforts of medicine and corneal transplants. I remember us all waiting for that phone to ring with news that there was a cornea available, but, for whatever reason, the transplant never succeeded. Today it would be a different story, I am sure.

Through all of this, Dad's spirit was indomitable and he was an incredible example of fortitude and determination. He never learned Braille, used a dog or cane—only dark glasses—because, I am sure, he never wanted to admit defeat. He just knew he would see again. Maybe it was pride. It was probably all of that and more.

Even after all these years, I can see him right now, being pleased as punch about how my life has turned out. He was quite a role model.

■ ■ ■

Cathleen Black is president of Hearst Magazines, a portfolio of titles that includes Cosmopolitan, Good Housekeeping, O, the Oprah Magazine, Harper's Bazaar, Town and Country, and fourteen others.

Jim Black was an independent food broker and ran a company that produced a line of specialty food items that would be found in gourmet food departments today. He was a great storyteller, loved life and, most of all, loved his family.

Eliza Bolen

■ OSCAR DE LA RENTA

PEOPLE KNOW my stepfather as a talented fashion designer. For nearly fifty years, Oscar de la Renta has been making beautiful, modern clothes that make women feel feminine and confident. To me, however, Oscar, so much more than a great designer and businessman (he has been my boss for the last ten years!), is above all a total optimist and lover of life.

Whether it is a family or business matter, he always sees the good in a situation, even if the news is the absolute worst! The day of my June garden wedding turned into a mini-monsoon. For six hours the lightning, thunder, and torrential downpour seemed like they would never end. Oscar, who along with my mother, had spent the previous months making sure that my dress, the tents, the flowers, and buffet tables would be perfect, simply smiled as the rest of us sank into depression. His positive manner calmed us all down as he reassured us that the rain would bring good luck to any marriage! By the end of our vows, the rain stopped, the clouds lifted, and the sun was shining. Oscar the optimist was right after all.

Alex and I have been happily married for years and our three beautiful sons simply adore Grandpa! From picking vegetables in his garden to teaching them prayers in Spanish, Oscar loves to be with the boys and show them new things. Of all the things our boys could learn from Grandpa, I hope that they learn to love life the way he does. Oscar is also one of the most gracious, caring, and generous individuals.

He has many strong passions—his family and friends, music, gardening, food, architecture, philanthropy, and traveling. I am always amazed how he can go on about these subjects! Oscar also has a wonderful knack for understanding people; he is never judgmental and he doesn't find fault. He believes in the basic goodness of people, and, accordingly, he's always willing to give someone a chance.

I feel so blessed to have Oscar in my life—he is a wonderful role model and my great friend. I am so happy that my mother married this incredible person. I hope that my boys can learn from their grandfather the way that I have.

■ ■ ■

Eliza Bolen is the Vice President of Licensing for Oscar de la Renta Ltd., a wife, and the mother of three boys.

Oscar de la Renta, a native of the Dominican Republic, has been designing his collection in New York since 1965. For over forty years, Oscar de la Renta's name has remained synonymous with elegance and style.

Cynthia Sidey Buck

■ HUGH SIDEY

I WAS BORN SEPTEMBER 3RD, on my dad's birthday. I always thought of him on our special day, especially when we were not together.

In my young adult years, while I was first in the working world or, as Daddy said, "gainfully employed," I labored over what to get my father for his birthday. It was important to me that I give something really special, something coveted, and something he greatly desired.

One year I knew he had an interest in a special pen, a black enamel fountain pen with a special gold quill tip. I searched and searched and finally found one in a tiny newspaper store on the upper east side of Manhattan. I was so excited to acquire this unique, and expensive, pen for my dad. He seemed equally as thrilled to receive it.

Another year it was a special bottle of brandy and two crystal brandy snifters, one of which shattered into a million pieces. I replaced it, and the new one also perished, in the dishwasher, suffering the element of very hot water with a chip and a large crack. Some things do not last forever.

Since having my children, I have come to learn some very valuable lessons about gift giving. It is the gifts from the heart that are the ones remembered forever. Daddy knew that too.

Although I know he appreciated the beautiful pen and the special brandy snifters, it was the simple gifts that inspired love of family and a heartfelt purpose.

The family tree my daughter, Bayly, made for him with cutouts of colorful paper on poster board, with all our family names and photographs as different branches of the tree, was primitive, though truly a beautiful gift, and an inspiration from a very young and happy heart.

My gift of a homemade peach pie (for lack of imagination or just wondering what my father could possibly want or need at that point in his life) inspired me to spend the afternoon of my birthday baking that special confection for his gift.

He absolutely loved it! It was I, however, that received the gift—a beautiful heartfelt thank-you note documenting every delicious bite of his gift.

After his passing, I had a whirlwind of emotions. In the quiet moments of the day, it is memories such as these that I cherish. His pleasure from receiving my homemade peach pie will bring a smile to my face every September 3rd.

■ ■ ■

Cynthia Buck lives in Chevy Chase, Maryland. A mother of three, she spends her time fundraising for various charities and organizations related to women and children.

Hugh Sidey was born in Greenfield, Iowa, and was a respected journalist working specifically on White House-related issues for Life and Time magazines. He passed away in the fall of 2005, and his presence will be missed by all that knew and loved him.

Barbara Bush

■ MARVIN PIERCE

SINCE I WAS ASKED to remember my dad, I have thought of so many happy times. My memories of my dad are all good. Next to my husband, Marvin Pierce was the most decent person I have ever met. He was really bright . . . worked his way through college, Phi Beta Kappa, nine-letter man at Miami University in Oxford, Ohio. He was funny and really wise.

I was the third of four children and was the recipient of his unconditional love. Now I realize that I was not his favorite child, but I thought that I was. I suspect that my sister and two brothers would tell you they were. He was that smart and that wise.

I went to the Milton School in Rye, New York, a public school quite far from our home. During the school year my dad and I walked fifteen minutes to Rye Station where my dad climbed on the train to go into NYC and I climbed on the bus to go to school. These were some of the happiest moments of my day. Daddy listened. (I called my father Daddy and my mother Mommy until I was married).

Daddy was a natural and put up with no fakes. As I was going out once with a boy, I said, "Good night, Father." He answered with, "Good night, Bobsy (which I hated), keep your nose clean." That humiliated me and certainly cured me of trying to put on airs . . . or at least with my dad!

My dad worked for the McCall Corporation and eventually became the CEO. He absolutely adored my beautiful mother and never criticized her or disagreed with her in any way. Well, I take that back. We lived in a small house and they had a tiny bathroom. That is where my mother's cairn dog, "Lassie," had her puppies. For six weeks after Lassie gave birth, I heard huge complaints about those pups.

Just before George and I were married my dad invited me to have lunch alone with him in the city. During this lunch he told me that he envied me. "The first year you are married is wonderful and it gets better with each following year." He said that he wished he could start all over with my mother. He went on to say that money problems were the causes of most divorces. I couldn't resist asking him how he could say that since my mother always had outstanding bills. "Don't go to Lord & Taylor's, Barbara, for your school clothes. I haven't paid the bill. Go to Best and Company." He laughed and said that he figured out early in their marriage that no matter how much money he budgeted for my mother she would spend more. So he gave her half of what he budgeted and then at Christmas time and maybe June he bailed her out. She thought he was a great hero and was so happy. He was that smart and that wise.

After my mother died, all sorts of antique dealers said that mother had put down payments on things and what were they to do? Daddy bought them all as that is what she would have done and he loved her.

I attended Smith College during WWII and really didn't get great grades as I really did not study as much as I should have. When my advisor, Miss Corwin, called my Phi Beta Kappa father, he made excuses: "Barbara's fiancé is overseas fighting the Japanese. I know she will do better." Not a case of being that smart, but of being very loving.

Daddy told me sometime in that period that there were only three things you really give your children.

1. The best education you can
2. Set a good example
3. All the love in the world

And I would add a fourth that George Bush has taught me. Trust your children, set them free, and give them independence.

I had the very best father ever.

■ ■ ■

Born *Barbara Pierce*, she grew up in Rye, New York, and attended Smith College. She married George H. W. Bush, who would become the 41st President of the United States, leading the way for her to champion family literacy.

Marvin Pierce was born in Dayton, Ohio, and attended Miami University in Oxford, Ohio, where he worked his way through school, graduated Phi Beta Kappa, and lettered in nine sports. He worked for the McCall Corporation, eventually as president, and passed away in 1969.

Rosanne Cash

■ JOHNNY CASH

WHEN I WAS eighteen years old and just graduated from high school, I took some time off before going to college to travel with my dad on the road. It was then that I learned to play guitar, and developed a passion for folk and country music, which up to that time I had eschewed as the music of my parents. On the bus one day, struggling with my new guitar skills (or lack thereof), he watched me for a few moments and then sat down and wrote a list of songs for me. In bold letters across the top of the page, he scrawled "100 Essential Country Songs." He handed me the list and told me that I needed to learn all these songs to complete my education. The list was far ranging and thorough; it was assembled from his intuitive understanding of each critical juncture in the evolution of country music. There were old Appalachian folk ballads and the songs of Jimmie Rodgers and Woody Guthrie. The influence of gospel and Southern blues was acknowledged, and he segued the list into rockabilly and then the birth of modern country music by way of Hank Williams, and up to the present, which was 1973. On the list were Carter Family songs like "Banks of the Ohio," Woody Guthrie songs like "This Land Is Your Land," history ballads like "The Battle of New Orleans," and Hank Williams's "I'm So Lonesome I Could Cry," as well as Carl Perkins's "Blue Suede Shoes." I endeavored to learn them all. I probably did, as the list hangs in front of me in my mind's eye to this day, thirty-three years later, and the songs became part of my background knowledge and source of reference when I began writing songs myself. I looked to that list as a standard of excellence, and to remind myself of the tradition of which I was a part.

Dad loved to talk politics almost as much as he loved to talk music. Interestingly, he had the same poetic grasp of world events as he had of the lexicon of American music. His understanding of the world was free of rigid ide-

ology, and full of an artist's sense of expansion, compassion, and a wider perspective that included the past, the future, and the human heart. The only subject on which he was unyielding was his belief in peace. He was a Southern Baptist who was nearly a Quaker in his absolute pacifism, but he was a true individual in how he expressed that belief. In the 1970s, he spoke out vociferously against the Vietnam War, and then immediately turned around and went there to play for the troops. This made a tremendous impression on my teenage brain, and I have endeavored ever since then to mold myself in the same spirit of personal truth, integrity, courage, and social activism with which he defined himself. That remarkable act, and the beliefs that informed it (which many thought to be the opposite of what they actually were), stands as a model of what I aspire to be in my most courageous version of myself.

In the last several years of his life, he developed a near-obsession with watching CNN, and he was always incredibly well informed. He intuitively understood what was not part of the headlines: the complexities and the backstories of various issues and conflicts. He had thoughtful opinions, based on his own principles and love of democracy. He also had great passion in his opinions, and we loved nothing more than to settle in with each other for a long conversation about politics and the state of the world. In the last few years of his life he rose very early in the morning. Whenever I went to Nashville to visit him, I forced myself awake at 3:30 or 4 a.m. and went into his little office to have coffee with him. He turned on the news and we mulled over what had happened in the world overnight. Those early mornings, before the house was awake or the staff had arrived, are some of my fondest memories of being with him. It was still dark outside on the lake just beyond his window, he was alert and interested in the world, and we were alone for a precious couple of hours. After we had digested the news, he turned the television off and I read to him from Psalms or Proverbs, until he grew tired again and had to take the first of several naps for the day.

He is defined to me by his love of language, songs, his love of being himself and being in the world, and his dedication to service and peace. That, combined with his love of rhythm and silly jokes, made up a father who stands unequaled among men to me. Not a day goes by that I don't think of him, or think of something I would like to share with him, or long for his advice, which I didn't ask for nearly often enough. I gave up watching CNN after he died, because no one else could bring his poet's understanding to this difficult world, and, without the poetry, the news is just too hard to take.

Rosanne Cash is a Grammy-winning singer and songwriter who has released 12 albums over the course of her 28-year career and had 11 number one records, as well as numerous awards for songwriting and performance. She is also a noted author and essayist whose prose has appeared in *The* New York Times, New York Magazine, *The* Oxford-American, Martha Stewart Living, *and various other periodicals and collections.*

Johnny Cash is one of the most beloved musicians in the history of American music, and is known to billions of people around the world. He is the winner of multiple Grammy awards and hundreds of other music awards, as well as the Medal of Arts, and is the only performer who was elected to all three Halls of Fame: the Rock and Roll Hall of Fame, the Country Music Hall of Fame, and the Songwriters Hall of Fame.

Alice Chandler

■ HAL PRICE HEADLEY

I WAS THE FOURTH of five daughters. The son came along eleven years after me! And whether my father intended it or not, I grew up as a boy and loved every minute of it!

My father owned almost 3000 acres of land, Beaumont Farm, and raised tobacco, cattle, and thoroughbred horses. If my toe was not under his heel, I was running way behind. He never said, "Al, don't do that, you might get hurt," and I tried it all!

Smokey Saunders won the 1935 Kentucky Derby, Preakness, and Belmont, and the Triple Crown, on Omaha. He came to work for Daddy and we became friends, shooting craps on the floor in the tack room at lunchtime. One day I got hot, made many passes, and ended up winning Smokey's car and $600 from him. Of course, I went home and bragged that night at dinner—Daddy made me give it all back! That was the last time that I told him everything!

He tried many times to win the Kentucky Derby. In 1938 he ran Menow, the best two-year-old colt of 1937. He and my mother took my sister Patricia and me to Churchill Downs that May of 1938 with the understanding that we would not say a word from the time we left Beaumont until after the race. That included an 85-mile drive, picnic lunch in Cherokee Park, and all of the races before the Derby.

Being superstitious, Daddy braided my brother Price's hair into Menow's foretop with navy blue and white ribbon, his racing colors. Menow led for a mile and finished fourth. The hair and ribbon were gone when he came back. After things quieted down that evening, Daddy sent the barn crew out to look for it. They found it at the quarter pole, where Menow lost the lead.

Daddy was responsible for the idea of Keeneland Racecourse, and for its building. It opened in 1936. I was with him most every day that I could be during that time when school permited. Keeneland is one of the world's greatest racecourses.

Daddy died at Keeneland in 1962. He had been having some heart trouble. He had just come up from Georgia where he wintered his horses for the Keeneland spring meet. We had worked them all. I was clocking from the stand; he was running up and down the honeysuckle bank at the 5/8 pole. We sat in the tack room and discussed the works. He got up without saying a word, and walked down the shed, speaking to his men and looking at the horses. Coming back, he dropped dead two stalls from the tack room, in front of a filly named Trouble Spot, which my son Mike was holding to have bandages put on her. He had dropped the latch on the tack room door, and I was locked in. After that, life was never the same.

■ ■ ■

Alice Chandler owns Mill Ridge farm, a thoroughbred horse farm in Lexington, Kentucky, which raises horses to race and sell. Mill Ridge raised Giacomo, the 2005 Kentucky Derby winner, and also sold a colt that brought $9.7 million to set a September sale record while becoming the third most expensive thoroughbred in history to sell at public auction.

Hal Price Headley was born in 1888 in Lexington, Kentucky. He was co-founder and first president of Keeneland Racetrack. He provided Mom the foundation broodmare, Alcibiades, whose great-granddaughter, Attica, would produce Sir Ivor, winner of the 1968 Epsom Derby, only the 3rd American bred to win in 200 runnings.

Elaine L. Chao

■ James S. C. Chao

MY FATHER has always been there for me. That is the first and foremost thought that comes to mind when I'm asked about my father.

As a young man, my father saw his birthplace ravaged by war and natural disasters. Yet his courage for life and belief in the basic goodness of people were never lost. In the aftermath of the civil war in China, my father relocated to Taiwan. There he met my mother, got married, and they started a family. My mother and father harbored the dream of one day immigrating to America to pursue greater opportunities for themselves and their children.

They made their dream come true. My father arrived in America first. It took him three long years before he could bring my mother, sisters, and me to the United States. During those years of separation, he and my mother communicated only through letters. Yet their love remained steadfast and loyal.

When my mother, sisters, and I finally arrived in America, I entered the third grade not speaking a word of English. Every day, I copied whatever was on the blackboard into my notebook. Every night, after his long and exhausting day of work, my father sat with me at the kitchen table, trying to decipher my childish scribbles so he could explain that day's lessons to me. That was how I learned English! Dad was patient, loving, and tireless as he and my mother built a new life for our family in this great country.

In the initial years after our arrival, my father held three jobs to make ends meet. Even so, he always made time for us. On the weekends, my father always took the whole family to the many free activities in New York City so that we could expand our horizons and learn more about our new country. Before the existence of "Take Your Daughters to Work Day," my father was already taking us to work with him on school holidays, so that we could understand what he did when he "went to work" every day.

At home, we were expected to help with household chores. My father was quite handy and he enjoyed fixing things around the house long after he could afford to pay someone else to do the job. When repairs or maintenance work were needed, he did it himself and had one of his daughters follow him around as a helper. I still remember those weekend afternoons as I followed my father around helping him with the chores. In watching him fix things, I acquired handy skills such as how to fix pipes and drains, paint the house, and tar the driveway, just to name a few. As my sisters and I took turns accompanying my father during his chores, he relayed stories of his childhood in China, his parents, the village where they lived, and the philosophical thinking of the "old country." The precious memories of those times together and those stories inspire me to this day.

As you can tell, our initial years in America were challenging and difficult. Nevertheless, my parents were always hopeful, optimistic, and forward looking. They never gave up their belief in the promise of America. They imbued their children with a deep sense of the possibilities in this country, if we worked hard and stayed focused. And, they taught us the importance of contributing to our community and our country.

My parents are great patriots. As a young couple in their 20s, they sacrificed everything that was near and dear to them—their family, friends, culture, language, and traditions—to start a new life in America so their children could have the best opportunities. It's people like my parents who make America great.

■ ■ ■

Elaine L. Chao was formerly President and CEO of United Way of America and director of the Peace Corps. As Secretary of Labor, she was the first Asian American woman ever appointed to a President's Cabinet in our country's history,

Dr. James S. C. Chao is a successful entrepreneur whose courage in coming to America and forging a new life for his family is an inspiration to all. A visionary and respected community leader, he and his wife, Ruth Mu-Lan Chu Chao, are rich in life's greatest treasures—family, faith, and love.

Mary Higgins Clark

■ LUKE JOSEPH HIGGINS

I WAS ELEVEN YEARS OLD when my father died in his sleep of a heart attack, and all these decades later never a day goes by that I don't think of him.

On Cape Cod, the early settlers called it the "tortience," that special bond which exists between a father and daughter. My father, Luke Joseph Higgins, was born in Roscommon, Ireland, and came to the United States in 1905 when he was twenty-one. I have the record of his arrival at Ellis Island that states he had five pounds in his pocket. Ten years later he became an American citizen. In those days he had to swear that he was neither an anarchist nor a polygamist and that he renounced his loyalty to George V, king of England.

The time I had with him was all too limited. Looking back, I'm glad that I had severe childhood asthma and frequently missed school. When the attacks came, I'd spend a good part of the night wheezing and gasping for breath, but, in the morning, the asthma eased off, and I'd go downstairs to share brunch with him. He owned a bar and grill which meant that he slept late in the morning, came home for an early dinner with the family, and then drove back to "the place" until three in the morning. The only evening in my life that I remember him being at home was just before he died. He had left work early because he didn't feel well.

A certain scent still reminds me of his shaving lotion. Phrases of songs he sang to me, off-key if my aunt Agnes was to be believed, still run through my mind. "Sunday night is my delight . . ." That's all I can remember. The rest of the words are gone.

My memory of his physical appearance remains vivid. He was a man just under six feet tall with thinning hair and a strong face. He had a quiet voice. "'Tis, dear," was the way he answered my questions in the affirmative.

Like the brother and sister who came to the United States within a year or two of him, he did not have a brogue, just a few expressions and a lilt in his voice that was the gift of his Irish ancestry. Years ago I met an elderly cousin who was the son of my father's oldest sister. "I looked like Luke when I was growing up," he explained. "And as your granddad got older he would call me Luke. Your dad was his favorite."

I remember standing in the backyard with him, shortly before he died, as he pointed to a dirigible floating overhead. It was the Hindenberg, and my father explained that it was the new way people would travel long distances. It exploded minutes later in one of the most famous disasters of the twentieth century. I still remember standing beside him and the feeling of protection I had from his presence as we looked at the giant object floating above us. After he died I had a heart hunger for that feeling that never abated.

My mother and father were married fourteen years when Daddy died. Joseph was thirteen, I was eleven, and John was seven. Years later that sad history repeated itself. My husband, Warren, died of a heart attack after we had been married fourteen years. Our five children ranged in age from five to thirteen. I understood everything they would be missing without their father because I had been there. Forty-one years later their memory of him is as fresh as mine is of my dad.

My father always wanted to go back to Ireland for a visit but never made it. There was never that much time to get away from the bar and grill.

Twenty-five years after his death I visited Ireland for the first time. The house where he had been raised is gone but the barn with its old oak door was still there. My father had told me how he and his brothers and sisters carved their names into that door. I found his name "Luke" and ran my finger over it. At that moment I felt as though I had not made that visit for him but with him. I looked over those beautiful green hills and whispered, "It's lovely here, Daddy."

I felt as though I was hearing him whisper back, "'Tis, dear."

■ ■ ■

Mary Higgins Clark is the author of twenty-four suspense novels; three collections of short stories; a historical novel, Mount Vernon Love Story; *and a memoir,* Kitchen Privileges; *and is the coauthor with Carol Higgins Clark of three Christmas suspense novels. More than eighty million copies of her books are in print in the United States alone, and her books are worldwide bestsellers. She lives in Saddle River, New Jersey, with her husband John Conheeney.*

Luke Joseph Higgins, died at 54 and six decades later is still alive to her.

Hillary Rodham Clinton

■ HUGH RODHAM

THE DAY AFTER my speech in Austin, my father died.
   I couldn't help but think of how my relationship with my father had evolved over time. I adored him when I was a little girl. I eagerly watched for him from a window and ran down the street to meet him on his way home after work. With his encouragement and coaching, I played baseball, football, and basketball. I tried to bring home good grades to win his approval. But as I grew older, my relationship with him inevitably changed, both because of my experiences growing up, which occurred in such a different time and place from his, and because he changed. He gradually lost the energy that got him outside throwing football pass patterns to me and Hugh as we ran around the elm trees in front of our house. Just as those magnificent elms succumbed to disease and had to be cut down in neighborhoods like ours throughout the country, his energy and spirit seemed to wane over time.

   More and more, his immediate world seemed to shrink as he lost his father and both brothers in a few short years in the mid-sixties. Then he decided in the early seventies that he had made and saved enough money, so he quit working and dismantled his small company. During my high school and college years, our relationship increasingly was defined either by silence, as I searched for something to say to him, or by arguments, which I often provoked, because I knew he always engaged with me over politics and culture—Vietnam, hippies, bra-burning feminists, Nixon. I also understood that, even when he erupted at me, he admired my independence and accomplishments and loved me with all his heart.

   I recently reread letters he wrote to me when I was at Wellesley and Yale, usually in response to a despondent collect call home in which I expressed doubts about my abilities or confusion about where my life was heading. I doubt anyone meeting my father or being on the receiving end of his caustic criticism would ever have imagined the tender love and advice he offered to buck me up, straighten me out, and keep me going.

I also respected my father's willingness to change his views, although he rarely admitted he had. He started out in life inheriting every prejudice imaginable in his working-class, Protestant family—against Democrats, Catholics, Jews, blacks, and anyone else considered outside the tribe. When I got exasperated by these attitudes during our summer visits to Lake Winola, I would announce to all the Rodhams that I intended to grow up and marry a Catholic Democrat—a fate they considered the worst I could meet. Over time, my father softened and changed, largely because of personal experiences with all kinds of people. He owned a building in downtown Chicago with a black man whom he came to respect and admire, causing him to change his views on race. When I grew up and fell in love with a Southern Baptist, my father was bewildered, but he rallied and became one of Bill's strongest supporters.

When my parents moved to Little Rock in 1987, they bought a condo next door to the one owned by Larry Curbo, a nurse, and Dr. Dillard Denson, a neurologist. They were among my mother's closest friends and began checking in on my parents, visiting with my dad, talking about the stock market or politics, and helping out my mother around the house. When Bill and I came to visit, the military and Secret Service used their house as the command center. One night my parents were watching a television show that featured gay characters. When my father expressed his disapproval of homosexuals, my mother said, "What about Dillard and Larry?"

"What do you mean?" he asked.

So my mother explained to my father that his dear friends and neighbors were a gay couple in a long-lasting committed relationship. One of my father's last stereotypes fell. Larry and Dillard visited my father in the hospital as he lay in a coma. One night Larry relieved my mother for a few hours so she could go home and get some rest. And it was Larry who held my father's hand and said good-bye as he died. Perhaps fittingly, my father spent his last days at St. Vincent's, a wonderful Catholic hospital, a sign that another of his prejudices had disappeared.

Early the next morning, Bill, Chelsea, and I, joined by an intimate group of family and friends, flew back to Little Rock for a memorial service at the First United Methodist Church. With us were my brother Tony, his future wife Nicole Boxer, my dear friend Diane Blair, who had been staying with us, Bruce Lindsey, Vince Foster, and Webb Hubbell. I was touched that Al and Tipper flew down with Mack McLarty, one of Bill's best friends from growing up and now White House Chief of Staff, along with Mack's wife Donna. The church on that Good Friday was filled for "A Service of Death and Resurrection" led by the church's senior minister, the Reverend Ed Matthews, and the minister who had married Bill and me, the Reverend Vic Nixon. After the service, our family, joined by Dillard and Larry, Carolyn, and Dr. John Holden, one of my brother's best friends from Park Ridge, took my father home to Scranton. In character, my father had chosen and paid for his gravesite years before.

We had a second funeral service at the Court Street Methodist Church, down the street from the house where my dad had grown up. Bill delivered a loving eulogy that conveyed Hugh Rodham's brusqueness and devotion:

> In 1974 when I made my first political race, I ran in a congressional district where there were a lot of Republicans from the Middle West. And my future father-in-law came down in a Cadillac with an Illinois license plate; never told a living soul I was in love with his daughter, just went up to people and said, "I know that you're a Republican and so am I. I think Democrats are just one step short of communism, but this kid's all right."

We laid him to rest in the Washburn Street Cemetery. It was a cold, rain-drenched April day, and my thoughts were as gloomy as the leaden sky. I stood listening to the Military Honor Guard's bugler playing taps. After the burial, we went with some of my father's old friends to a local restaurant, where we reminisced.

We were supposed to be celebrating my father's life, but I was overwhelmed with sadness for what he would now be missing. I thought about how much he enjoyed seeing his son-in-law serve as president and how much he wanted to watch Chelsea grow up. When Bill was preparing his eulogy on the plane from Little Rock, we were all telling stories. Chelsea reminded us that her PopPop had always said that, when she graduated from college, he would rent a big limousine and pick her up wearing a white suit. He had many dreams that wouldn't be realized. But I was thankful for the life, opportunities, and dreams he passed along to me.

Hillary Rodham Clinton was elected to the Senate in 2000. She is the first and only First Lady to be elected to any federal office and the first New York Senator to sit on the Senate Armed Services Committee. Since her election, Senator Clinton has been a strong and tireless advocate for New York, dedicated to protecting the security and prosperity of New York's communities.

Hugh Rodham was born in Scranton, Pennsylvania, and later enlisted in the Navy. After serving for several years, he settled down in Chicago, where he started a small drapery fabric business and, with Dorothy Rodham, raised three children.

Nadia Comaneci

■ GHEORGHE COMANECI

DID YOU MISS OUT on a "normal" childhood? How much did you have to sacrifice to become a gymnastics champion? These are questions that I still get asked every day.

Of course, because I was so committed to gymnastics as a child, I missed out on a certain amount of time with my family, but the quality of time we spent together was what I most cherish.

Our family was typical of most working-class families during the Communist era in Romania. So, I was extremely fortunate that my family supported me and allowed me to follow my dreams of becoming a gymnastics champion. Sure, it was a lot of hard work, but it was easy compared to the sacrifices that my father made to provide for our family every day.

My father, Gheorghe Comaneci, grew up in the small village of Harja, in the foothills of the Carpathian Mountains of Romania. At six feet four inches tall, he is a strong but gentle man and he is as tough as they come.

My father does not use many words, but the strength and conviction behind his words are clear. This is an aspect of my father's personality that, even today, deeply influences my attitude and behavior.

I'll never forget the intense media scrutiny of me after I earned the first score of perfect 10 in the 1976 Olympics in Montreal. Every time I turned my head there was a reporter sticking a microphone in front of my face asking questions. I was just fourteen years old. How could I have realized what I had just accomplished? Thus, I did not have much to say.

So, when I was asked if I was surprised at my performance, I said, "No, I am not surprised. I worked hard for this and, actually, I have done better in practice." Some observers thought I was arrogant, or flippant. That was not the case at all. This short, matter-of-fact comment was exactly what my father would have said . . . a few truthful words, with no nonsense, and a very clear meaning.

My father was an auto mechanic who walked nearly twelve miles a day to and from work. He smelled of oil, and yet he never owned his own car and had no desire to— cars, he used to say, always break down.

I admire, and respect, my father, and there was never any question that I was "Daddy's girl."

Like most young girls, when I was about twelve years old, I desperately wanted a pair of roller skates. My mother said we didn't have money to buy them. I refused to accept her answer, so I convinced my father to come with me to the store, just to try the skates on—the old divide and conquer scheme. Once the skates were on my feet and I could feel the speed and power as I sped through the store, I couldn't bear to give them back. I raced onto the street wearing them so that my father was forced to buy them. I have never been able to take "no" as an answer. This I got from my father, as well.

However, one time I pushed my luck a little too far, and that is when I discovered my father's real strength and love for me.

This was the one and only time in my life that my father spanked me. I was seven years old. One morning, on my own, I decided to play outside all day, so I ran out the door and found some other children who wanted to spend the day running through the forests and scrambling up trees. I didn't return home until after dark that night.

We didn't have telephones in our homes, and I didn't check in with my parents all day. My father was frightened on the night I came home after dark because he thought I'd been hurt. There had been a rumor that a dead child had recently been discovered in the basement of a home in a neighboring town. When I walked into the house whistling, like a happy-go-lucky girl, my father was waiting for me by the window, and he was furious. He spanked me once with his belt on my behind, and, as you can imagine, I never did anything like that again!

To this day, people still ask me about scoring the perfect 10 in gymnastics, and yes, it was exciting, but it was merely the result of the hard work and dedication that I learned from my father.

Gheorghe retired several years ago, but recently he started a new small business where he produces pickled vegetables and sells them in the farmer's market. Because he is the owner of his new company, I call him "Mr. President." I still admire and love him very much.

■　■　■

Nadia Comaneci earned the first perfect 10 score in the history of Olympic gymnastics competition on her way to winning a total of nine Olympic medals, five of them gold.

Gheorghe Comaneci retired from his work as an auto mechanic, and currently runs a pickling business in the farmer's market in Onesti, Romania.

*Mary Cooley Craddock
Susan Cooley King,
Louise Cooley Davis
Helen Cooley Fraser*

■ DENTON COOLEY

In memory of our sister, Florence Talbot Cooley

OVER A TEN-YEAR PERIOD, our father received news that his wife, Louise, had delivered another baby . . . girl. Mary, Susan, Louise, Florence, and Helen—five healthy baby girls. When we daughters started having our own children, there were five granddaughters in a row. Thinking he was genetically jinxed, our father was in total disbelief in 1993 to hear that a BOY had finally been born. Daddy rushed straight to the newborn nursery and ripped into the diaper to see the evidence. He couldn't believe this "girl streak" had been broken. That child inherited the Name, Denton Arthur Cooley Walker. Daddy was so excited that he suggested the last name, Walker, be dropped!

Daddy loved his daughters and treated us no differently than if we had been boys. He only required we NOT use his razor to shave our legs. He didn't want to raise dependent girls, so we all have learned to fend for ourselves. For example, it was not unheard of to jump in the car for school and realize that the tires were flat; so we learned to change tires, quickly. He required that we learn to drive stick-shift cars so we would never be stranded on a date.

While my mother did the day-to-day childrearing, our father was good natured and interested in our activities. He inspired us by his own example.

He worked all day, every day. But, when he came home he was ready to play tennis, go to ballet or piano recitals, or drive us all to Cool Acres, our farm, or the "ski shack" on the San Jacinto River. It was still hard work for him, saddling horses or getting us up on water skis, and few other men have his stamina. The key was that both weekend spots were within 45 minutes of town so he could return for emergencies at the hospital. He was able to make rounds on his patients on Sunday morning and spend quality time with his family in the afternoon.

The constant challenge at the "ski shack" was to launch the boat and start the motor. The seldom-used boat engine often refused to fire up. Daddy never lost his cool at this frustration. He was determined not to waste an afternoon. We learned all sorts of tricks to tweak the spark plugs or dry out the carburetor. Perseverance, prayer, and a squirt of Hot Shot were the formula to get that motor purring. Just like getting a patient's heart beating in surgery, he patiently tried all remedies to save our day of fun.

Skiing on the San Jacinto River required skill and bravery. A passing barge could suck us under if we fell in the middle, or a swarm of water moccasins would eat us alive if we dropped too near the shore. And, if we took too long trying to get up on the skis, the polluted water would make us radioactive. He would not have a bunch of sissies on his hands, so we learned to beach start and hold on tight to the slalom rope, muscles cramping, until we finally reached the sandy shore, where we would glide up on the river's sandbar beach.

And the final task of getting the boat out of the river was a feat that only the toughest of girls could handle. Three in the oily water guided the boat onto the trailer, while Daddy cranked the winch, and another of us floored the station wagon accelerator. Burning rubber, the boat and trailer were yanked up the slippery launch ramp. It was dangerous, exciting, and greatly satisfying at the end of the day.

Our father became world famous for his feats in heart transplantation and innovations in heart surgery. With him, we got to meet many celebrities, like presidents of Italy, Jordan, the United States, and Spain, and Pope Paul VI. It was so special growing up with a well-known and respected dad who was witty, positive, generous, and kind. All girls should be so lucky!

■ ■ ■

Mary Cooley Craddock is a medical illustrator and mother of six; Susan Cooley King is a pediatric nurse practitioner, director of Texas's child literacy program, and a mother of four; Louise Cooley Davis, M.D. is an ophthalmologist, accomplished golfer, and mother of two; Florence Talbot Cooley is deceased; and Helen Cooley Fraser is the wife of a heart surgeon and mother of four.

Dr. Denton Cooley is a cardiovascular surgeon who is famous for performing the first U.S. heart transplant and implanting the first artificial heart in a human. He is a pioneer in his field, has performed more heart operations than any other physician, and has trained 900 young heart surgeons. He is the father of five daughters.

Barbara Hoffa Crancer

■ JAMES RIDDLE HOFFA

AT 7:30 A.M. on July 31, 1975, I answered the telephone to hear my mother say, "Your father did not come home last night." I knew at that moment that I would never see my father again. After a frantic few hours I sank into my seat on an airplane and closed my eyes. I had a vision of my father dressed in dark pants and a short-sleeved, dark shirt. His body was slumped over as if dead. I had no way of knowing that these were the clothes he wore when he disappeared. I flew to Detroit to take care of my mother as my father had instructed me to do all my life.

My father was strong both physically and mentally. He taught me many lessons as a child to foster these qualities in me as if he knew in the future I would need them.

One of the first lessons I remember is having the job of placing his long-distance phone calls from home. This required speaking to the operator to tell her the phone number and the person to whom my father wished to speak. When the person came on the line, I was taught to say in my little-girl voice, "Please hold for Mr. Hoffa." In this way my father taught me to be comfortable speaking to others.

Once when I was small we were walking together on a cold, Michigan winter day. I was complaining about the cold. My father said, "You can feel it, can't you, sister? When you are dead you won't feel a thing." I hear those words whenever I walk in the cold and remember how good it is to be alive and feel the cold.

As my father rose in the leadership of the Teamsters, many times he was out of town from Monday to Friday. My mother never drove a car so weekends were busy with errands. My brother and I accompanied him. By the time I was eight or ten he was a recognized figure in Detroit. I was always proud when a clerk or worker would say, "Hey, Jim! Keep up the good work." My father always took the time to talk to people and listen to their problems. If he could help, he did.

I was told a story to illustrate his empathy for a person in need of help and his uncanny ability to see a problem and decide the solution on the spot. He was attending a union meeting in a Southern state and as he left the hall a woman approached. She told him that her husband had been a union truck driver and was recently killed on the job. She needed a job to support her children. The officers of the local would not help her. Dad asked the president of the local if this was true and he said, "Yes." My father said to several officers in the group, "Give me your wallets." He took all their money and the contents of his own wallet and gave it to the woman. He said, "You call this man tomorrow and, if you don't have a job in two weeks, you call me."

Both my parents knew what it was to be poor. They lived through the Depression and World War II. Once I recall my father saying, "Remember, where there is no money there is no love." I rejected the thought as harsh and wrong. As I have grown older I have come to understand that he was not speaking literally. He just knew how hard it is to be happy when you cannot pay the rent or feed or clothe your children. This is why he fought all his life to achieve for the worker a decent wage and standard of living.

At my wedding in October 1961, my father wore a tuxedo for the first time in his life. I know that he attended many black tie functions before that date and refused to wear one as not befitting a labor leader. We also danced the father-daughter dance. He had never danced with my mother. She was astonished.

My father, James R. Hoffa, taught me by example what it means to be a good human being who cares about others. His life was dedicated to the labor movement. Teamster members benefit today from his dedication. For this I celebrate his life.

■ ■ ■

Barbara Hoffa Crancer was born and raised in Detroit, Michigan. She was appointed Associate Circuit Judge for the State of Missouri in July of 1992 after graduating from Washington University School of Law in St. Louis, Missouri, in 1985.

James Riddle Hoffa was born in Brazil, Indiana and relocated to Detroit, Michigan, after the death of his father. He left school at the age of 14 to support his family. He became a member of the Teamsters Union at age 16, rising to the presidency in 1957 at the age of 44.

Paula Creamer

■ PAUL CREAMER

PAUL. PAULA. The fact that I'm named after my dad kind of says it all. According to my mom, we are pretty much identical—intense, competitive, and at times even a little stubborn. My dad is loving, supportive of everything that I do, hard on me when he needs to be, and of course my biggest fan. We have this fantastic relationship that really solidified when, appropriately enough, we started playing golf together.

Before I played golf I was a gymnast. My dad wasn't going to curl my hair or help me put on my makeup (my mom took care of that), so he was limited in his involvement. Then about seven years ago, my dad tore his Achilles tendon. After the injury, he was able to spend even more time with me. We played a lot of golf. He, of course, blamed any loss on the boot he had to wear for his torn tendon! I think that his injury was a blessing in disguise because of how close we became.

Eventually I had to choose between cheerleading and golf. I talked to my mom and dad about the decision I had to make and my dad asked me, "Well, Paula, would you rather cheer for people or have people cheer for you?" He would have been happy with whatever I had chosen. I chose golf.

Since that decision, my parents have made many sacrifices for me. My dad is a former Navy pilot and now flies for American Airlines. When I was given the opportunity to attend the David Leadbetter Golf Academy in Bradenton, Florida, my dad asked American for a transfer from San Francisco to Miami and moved my family down there so that I could pursue my dreams. I know that relocating the family was a tough decision, and I am forever grateful for having such supportive parents.

A pretty good golfer himself, my dad has taught me a lot about the game.

In teaching me the rules of golf, my dad also taught me to play by those rules and to respect them. I have called penalties on myself for small infractions like letting the club touch the sand in a bunker shot, but was presented with my biggest challenge this past fall. I was playing in the Office Depot Championship and bad weather had delayed the final two holes until that Monday morning. My dad asked me if I wanted to adjust the setup of my bag since I would not need my 3-wood on the last two holes—a par 3 and a par 4. So we took out the 3-wood and put in a stronger 5 iron (which I ended up not using anyway!) and I finished the tournament in 23rd place, earning a check for $11,859. Later on that day we drove out to San Diego to meet with my sponsors and agent and somehow the story came up about switching the clubs. My agent said, "Paula, you can't do that!" You see, we didn't know it was against the rules. So, we talked about it for a few minutes and I immediately called the rules officials to inform them of what I had—accidentally—done. I was ultimately disqualified from the tournament. I think that my dad was a little embarrassed by the situation but was really proud that I had displayed integrity in being honest about my mistake. We joke about it now. Dad asks me randomly, "So, Paula, do you want to change the setup of your bag?" I laugh and joke back, "That's why you'll never caddie for me, Dad!"

My dad has actually caddied for me a few times, and we have a funny inside joke that came out of one of those experiences. I was playing in Tulsa at John Q. Hammons and was setting up a 50-yard pitching shot on the 13th hole. As I hit the shot, I could tell that it was going to be a little short, so I automatically reacted, "Go, go, go," coaxing the ball. My dad heard me and started chiming in, "Go, go, go . . . that's going to be short, go!" I turned to him and said, "Don't ever talk to my golf ball like that again!" Now he says all kinds of things like, "GET DOWN," or "GO, GO, GO" or "SIT, SIT DOWN," or "BITE, BITE, Come on, BITE!" He drives me crazy when he does that but I know that he is just really excited and wants the best for me. It still bugs me though and I get mad at him and tell him, "Don't talk to my golf balls." He laughs and starts walking to the ball.

My dad has also taught me to be different and has always told me to be who I want to be. He knew that I loved pink (I have pink tees, clothes, golf shafts) and that I wanted something pink for my bag. So we went into a pro shop one afternoon and my dad picked out this bright, neon pink pig head cover for my clubs! I mean, this thing was the brightest shade of pink I'd ever seen. I said with a concerned face, "I don't know if I can use this, Dad . . . It's just too pink!" He replied, "Yeah, you can do it; don't worry what people think." So I used the pink pig in the tournament the next day and ended up winning. My dad and I gave credit to the pig, and since then I've had four pink pigs. Each time one pig faded because of the sun, my dad came home with a new one. He sits the old pink pig in front of the new one and has the old pig tell the new one that he'd better do a good job or he is going to have to replace him! Now I have a pink panther on my bag and have gotten the nickname "The Pink Panther," and the funny part is that my dad kind of started the whole thing!

I am so lucky to have such a wonderful relationship with both of my parents. Before I start each round, I have to find my parents so that I can give them a hug and a kiss. They always say, "We love you, good luck, play hard." We also end each round with a hug and a kiss. I won't start the round until my parents and I have hugged, and it's actually gotten harder to find them now that I'm no longer in amateur tournaments, but I always do! They are the first and last thing that I think about whenever I play, and even though I'm growing up (even though my dad would like to prevent that from happening!), my parents will continue to be the most important people in my life!

■ ■ ■

Paula Creamer grew up in Pleasantown, California. She learned to play golf at Castlewood Country Club with her dad because their home overlooked the first hole. She went on to become the youngest winner of a multiple round golf tournament in the 53-year history of the Ladies Professional Golf Association.

Paul Creamer grew up in Liverpool, NY. He learned to fly in the Navy after he graduated from the U.S. Naval Academy in Annapolis, MD. After 22 years of naval service he retired from the Navy as a captain and currently flies for American Airlines. Paula is very proud of him and knows that her various opportunities and successes are a result of her father's love and sacrifice.

Bo Derek

■ PAUL COLLINS

THIS PAST DECEMBER my father turned 75 years old. Surely a marker to celebrate, and for my whole life I couldn't remember ever having a birthday party for him. I called my brother and two sisters to organize a surprise dinner at his favorite Italian restaurant, where we were to give him all kinds of clever and funny gifts and a big cake with a picture of him as a young man that would somehow be laser printed with black and white frosting on the top of it. This would be very special, very personal.

I should have known better. A week before the big night, my brother told us that Dad would be out of town for his birthday.

So, as usual, on Christmas Day, after we all stuffed our bellies and opened our presents and felt like doing anything but celebrating all over again, we brought in the cake, tiredly sang "Happy Birthday" to my father and gave him yet another gift, this one marked "Happy Birthday" but wrapped in paper with Santas all over it. Such a sad, uninspired little celebration. The next morning I got up early to spend a little father–daughter time with my dad only to find his minivan gone, the guest bed stripped, and the sheets sitting in a neat ball on top of the washer.

That's my dad. He was on his way to Glamis to race dune buggies with his pals. Paul Johnson Collins. Post–greatest generation Korean War veteran left Southern Illinois and the prospect of working in the coal mines to come to the sunshine and opportunity of California.

My first memories of him are doing wheelies on a motorcycle in San Pedro where he worked on a big-rig dredge, building Los Angeles Harbor. He rode large, deep-rumbling, powerful bikes. And I remember being lifted up in front of him, straddling the gas tank and holding on to his arms. It made me feel very proud that I was riding with him. I loved the speed, the sound, and the wind in my hair. I hoped everyone would see us and notice. He was my dad!

He's always made quality of life his priority, sometimes sacrificing success in the business world. Considering the fact that at one time he sold Bibles door to door, he was lucky that most of his life he was able to work for whatever company made the toy he was into at the moment—from catamaran sailboats and windsurfers to monster trucks and, of course, motorcycles. He held positions from salesman to public relations manager, even high-powered corporate executive with an expense account, an avocado green Plymouth Charger, and a hard-sided Samsonite briefcase to match. So super-cool, so Steve McQueen-ish to all of us kids.

I used to think that eventually my father would grow up, become more responsible, like other men. But so far he is still true to himself. When he called me yesterday, his cheerful voice said, "Just calling to make sure you're having fun." A simple creed, and it works for him. He is so enormously rich in friends. Self-taught, still learning, and so damned interested in everything. Proud beyond words of his four children and six grandchildren. With a wanderlust, he never passes up an adventure and, I believe, has no regrets whatsoever.

Oh my, as I write this I realize . . . I'm so much like him.

■ ■ ■

Bo Derek is a film actress and producer.

Paul Collins is a California entrepreneur in the motorcycle and sailing business.

Elizabeth Dole

■ JOHN VAN HANFORD

MY DAD, John Van Hanford, was of the old school. His rock-solid values provided me with a blueprint for life, and his appreciation for America and her opportunities enriches me to this day. Dad gave me so many gifts over the years. An accomplished musician, he gave me the gift of music, which has brought so much joy to my life. He gave me the gift of education, which opened the world's door to my future. And, most importantly, he gave me the gift of integrity, which I keep with me every day.

Most simply put, Dad's word was his bond. He had respect for honesty and responsibility—and disrespect for their lack. For example, I can still hear him calling his physician, Dr. Fields, one day when his knee blew out. "Doc," he said, "I don't have time to come by, but sit down and put your hand on your knee." After describing his pain and receiving a diagnosis by phone, Dad insisted on getting billed for a visit.

Profoundly devoted to family, he also provided firm discipline. When my family moved into a new house that Dad had designed, I decided to paste thirteen valentines on the walls to enhance the decor. My father was not pleased with my new penchant for interior design.

He took me to each valentine and asked, "Who did this?"

At first, I blamed it on my imaginary playmate, Denaw.

"No," Dad said, "Denaw hasn't been here today."

"Johnny did it," I said, blaming my brother John, who is 13 years my senior and stands six feet, two inches tall.

"No, Johnny would have put them way up high," Dad replied.

Finally, I had to admit, "Elizabeth did it."

At each valentine, as I acknowledged responsibility, Dad gave me a few pats with a switch from the backyard hedge—a simple lesson in honesty I

have never forgotten. Of course the switch didn't cause much pain, but what hurt most was disappointing the man I loved so much.

As I grew up, my father always supported my interests and taught me that anything worth doing deserved my best effort. When I wanted to run for president of my high school, which girls didn't do in those days, he stood right behind me, cheering me on. He was protective but never overbearing, even when he had reservations about what I wanted to do. In 1959, while enjoying a summer study in England at Oxford University, I developed a hankering to visit the Soviet Union.

My father had one of Salisbury, North Carolina's more elaborate bomb shelters in our basement, indicative of his view of the Iron Curtain and the leaders behind it. Mother shared his feelings. I had tipped them off by letter about my planned trip, which prompted a resounding "No!" When the long-distance operator alerted them one night to a call from Oxford, they shook hands at the bottom of the staircase and took up battle stations at separate phones.

It was tempting fate, Dad told me, to be in the USSR when Nikita Khrushchev was coming to the United Nations. What if someone took a shot at Khrushchev while in New York? They'd lock up every American in Russia. But having learned persistence and thoroughness from my dad, I was ready to counter his objections. After a lively debate, he said, "If I were there, I'd go with you," conceding the educational benefits outweighed the dangers. Always the protective parent, Dad knew when to let go and allow me to expand my horizons.

This strong, godly, compassionate man—my beloved father—set the course for my life. His gifts are with me still; they'll be with me forever.

■ ■ ■

Elizabeth Dole's public service career includes two Cabinet positions as Secretary of Transportation and Secretary of Labor, president of the American Red Cross, and her current position, the senior senator and the first woman elected to the U.S. Senate from North Carolina.

John Van Hanford was a pioneer in the florist industry in the Southeast, rising from regional to national prominence in horticultural production, manufacturing, importing, and wholesale distribution of floral products, and as a commercial real estate developer.

Barbara Mandrell Dudney

■ IRBY MANDRELL

A FATHER AND DAUGHTER working together are a powerful combination.

My daddy was my personal manager during my thirty-eight-year career in the music business. I was so blessed to have a manager who had my best interest at heart in everything he did. After all these years, he was and still is my mentor and my hero.

Daddy is a man with integrity and wisdom, who taught me by example, dependability, and honesty. Many times I've heard him say, "A man's word is his bond. Do what you say you are going to do." He taught me to "always give people their money's worth."

Times were pretty tough when I first started recording and touring and it was Daddy who made "hangin' in there" possible for me. In those days, Daddy was not only my manager, but he also booked my dates, played a rhythm guitar, and sang backup in my band. He carried equipment in and out of venues, set up the sound system, and drove the bus twelve to eighteen hours a day. Whatever it took to get the job done, he did it.

Every Veteran's Day, I speak to my father and I give him a card to tell him how grateful I am for him and to say thank you for my freedom. During World War II, he joined the Navy at the age of seventeen. He became a corpsman and was assigned to "Landing Beach Party #4," and some other assignments during his military service. From the pictures I've seen, he sure looks handsome in a uniform. He wore another uniform again when he was a policeman in Corpus Christi, Texas, for five years.

My mother, Mary, and my father, Irby, had three daughters. I was the oldest, next is Louise, and then Irlene. They always said, "Eenie, Meenie, Miney, and no Mo." We three girls agree that we have the greatest father and mother in the world, and that none of us would have had our careers if we hadn't had them for our parents. Our family is very close, and there's nothing we wouldn't do for each other. That extreme love and closeness comes from the top—Daddy and Mother.

I want to share a little story that demonstrates how very clever Daddy has always been with me. I was six and the only child and very happy about that fact. When Daddy brought Mother and my new baby sister, that I definitely didn't want, home from the hospital, he came into the house, and appeared so very angry because he said the hospital had given us the wrong baby. "This is not our baby; it has black hair and it's just not ours, and I'm going to flush it down the toilet." He then went storming into the bathroom and locked the door. I could hear him jiggling the toilet handle, and I was crying and yelling, "No, give me the baby, she's my baby!" He opened the door and I took my new baby sister and held her close to me, and I loved her and never had a jealous moment, not ever. There was an old television show that I watched as a little girl called Father Knows Best. Well, in my case it's so true; my Daddy does know best.

■ ■ ■

Entertainer and country music legend Barbara Mandrell Dudney has received over seventy-five major awards in her career spanning almost forty years in the entertainment business. She heard many loving and encouraging words from her father, including "I'd bet my last penny on you."

Irby Mandrell managed his daughter's phenomenal career. At seventeen, he proudly served in the United States Navy during WWII. However, his most cherished accomplishments involve giving to his own family. In addition to being married for fifty-eight years to his loving wife Mary, he also managed the thriving careers of Louise and Irlene Mandrell.

Dianne Feinstein

■ LEON GOLDMAN

MY FATHER was a professor of surgery at the University of California Medical Center. And though I did not follow in his footsteps, I have tried to live up to his legacy of compassion and do my part in healing our nation.

So I want to share some of the great lessons he taught me, and which have formed the foundation of my career in public service:

■ **Be compassionate.** My father had a deep and compelling feeling for his patients. People have come up to me and said, "Your father has the Hands of God." He made a house call on everyone he operated on to see how they were afterwards and formed lifelong friendships with the people who were his patients.

■ **Treat the whole patient, not just the wound.** My father knew that you can't just treat the symptoms, but you need to look deeply to find solutions to underlying problems.

■ **Reduce a problem down to its basics.** Whether he was teaching medical students or helping me and my two sisters with our homework, my father had a knack for reducing an issue to its core and then helping work through the issue in a simple and understandable way.

■ **Never be satisfied.** My father had a will of iron. He taught me that, if you worked hard, there were no limits on what you could achieve. He used to say, "Get to your work a half hour early; don't take a coffee break; and be the last one out at night." When I held my first job in "Notions" at the Emporium Department Store at the age of sixteen, that's exactly what I did.

My father was a fine surgeon, a careful scholar, and a great teacher. He was a loyal friend and a proud father. I miss him deeply every day.

And when I see the power of compassion or hard work prove out, I think of my father and know that he would look on and smile.

■ ■ ■

Dianne Feinstein is the senior senator from California. She was born and raised in San Francisco.

Dr. Leon Goldman was a professor of surgery at the University of California Medical Center.

Wanda Ferragamo

■ FULVIO MILETTI

WHEN I FACE the reality of life, I send a message of gratitude to my father for the education and discipline he taught me. He was a medical doctor, he was a Catholic, and he made a mission of his profession. Everybody respected and loved him in the town where we lived.

He was strong and severe. He did not like too much effusion. Therefore, one day when I saw my granddaughter playing with her father, combing his hair and jumping on his shoulders, I regretted that I was not allowed to be so confidential with my father, too. Although I loved him, I am thankful to my mother for explaining to me and my brothers that he was a kind and wonderful person and how very much he cared for the family.

Anyway, I have some very nice memories of him that I deeply treasure. I remember, one day, I was six years old and I was crying. There were several members of my family all there, and in front of everybody I said, all of a sudden, "Nobody loves me! Mum loves Silvio (my brother) and Granny loves Tullio (my other brother). Nobody loves me!"

In that precise moment, I remember, my father opened his jacket, took me in his arms and said, "Daddy loves you!" and I became immediately happy and proud.

Of course, from then on I knew where to go when I needed to ask for something I wanted.

Another nice story comes to my mind. I was about seven or eight years old and, being that my father was a doctor, I took my three or four dolls to him pretending that something was wrong with them and he had to treat them.

So he asked me what was wrong with the dolls. He put the thermometer under their arms, moved the arms and legs in order to check if everything was functioning well. Then I was satisfied and I took them away in a little carriage. So, although he was a serious person, he had patience with my dolls.

Also I am very glad that I was able to put together many articles he wrote about many interesting, different subjects, and publish them in a small book in order to transmit to my children, and now to my grandchildren, his very special thoughts.

■ ■ ■

Wanda Ferragamo is president of the world-renowned Ferragamo fashion house. She and her children took over the business in 1960, when Salvatore, her husband and founder of Ferragamo, passed away at a young age.

Fulvio Miletti was born in 1880 and was father to four children, Wanda being the youngest. He dedicated his life to the practice of medicine in the city of Bonito.

Debbi Fields

■ EDWARD MARTIN SIVYER

THE YOUNGEST OF FIVE GIRLS, I already knew that I had let my dad down! He wanted a son. Yet, I arrived, an 8 pound, 12 ounce baby girl. No one would carry on the family name.

I wanted to be the son he never had. My dad loved to fish. So, I got up at dawn and we headed out to sea, many times in horrible weather conditions. When my dad wasn't fishing, we went up to the beach and went clam digging in the sand. I loved finding long-necked clams, but what I hated was eating them, or any type of seafood. Whatever we brought home, my mom would cook. And I dreaded dinner. I realized the only way to combat a terrible dinner was to whip up chocolate chip cookies. This way, I had something that I loved eating to look forward to.

The greatest gift I ever received from my dad was a fire engine–red bike. My dad was a welder, and had come across an old bike in the dump. He brought the bike frame home and told me he was going to make it brand spanking new! He welded the frame until it was a piece of art! I was thrilled, but did not know how to ride a bicycle. So, he showed me how to ride. As he pedaled away, the bike chains got off track and he fell very hard on the cement. I hated to see him hurt, but he was tough and did not complain. I was determined that I was going to learn how to ride my bike that night. I fell several times, but I learned! I learned that going through life and riding a bike are very similar. First, in order to get anywhere in life you have to look into the future to plan where you are going. Next, I learned the importance of not looking back. Moving forward, in a positive direction, will lead you to success. Sometimes, you hit a bump in the road and crash, as with life. I learned that the only failure is not to try. When you fall, you get back up, every time. I learned perseverance.

I wanted my dad's attention so badly; I listened to his dreams of getting

an aluminum fishing boat. He also dreamed of putting his camper on his truck and traveling America with my mom.

But, they were simply dreams without a date and time. He talked, but never acted on his dreams. This bothered me because I believed in dreams and, more importantly, I believed that they could come true! He encouraged each one of my sisters and me to seek something we love to do. Making, eating, and sharing chocolate chip cookies was something I absolutely loved to do!

There was one thing that drove me crazy about my dad. He always said he loved each of his girls equally. I asked him, "Dad, I want you to tell me that you love me, Debbi." His response was always, "Debbi, you know I love all my girls the same."

I tried so hard to show him I was worthy of his love. Besides being a tomboy, at thirteen, I worked for the Oakland A's as Charlie Finley's first female foul line ball catcher. At fifteen, I was working at a department store while going to school. I earned my own money to go on ski trips with my class and buy my own clothes. You name it. If I wanted to do or have something, I worked for it.

When I was sixteen, I became a professional water skier. I graduated high school at seventeen and enrolled in junior college. By the time I turned 20, I was married and decided to start my own cookie business. After some trying times, the cookie business became successful and we were beginning to get some notice. I could hardly wait for my dad's response. "Dad, are you proud of me? Did you read the news about my company?" He said, "Debbi, I am not interested in your business and I don't want to talk about it. If you want to talk about family, that is fine, but no business." I felt like no matter what I did, I was never going to get his individual attention.

The toughest part came when my dad was dying of colon cancer. He had all the obvious signs, but ignored them, missing out on a possible diagnosis and perhaps a cure. On his deathbed, I asked him to tell me he loved me, but he said simply that he loved all his girls equally. And so, he left this earth.

At his funeral, my sisters showed me his wallet. Inside, there was a picture of my mom and him on one of their many anniversaries, a picture of all his girls at the wedding of my sister, a picture of his most beloved dog, Dino, and at the very end, hidden in the very back, was a picture of . . . just me! (See bottom of page 79.) I always knew he loved and was proud of me, but he was never able to tell me. I cherish that moment, for it gave me an opportunity to bring closure to an open wound, which healed miraculously with knowledge. What did I learn from my dad?

- True wealth is found in family, true friends, and absolutely loving what you do!
- Money is never an indicator of wealth.
- Work hard, play hard.
- Dream big, and unlike my dad, take actions to make them happen.
- Be strong, be tough, and never complain.
- Tell the ones I love how much I love them and celebrate all the uniqueness that only exists in them.

Lucky me.

■ ■ ■

Debbi Fields continues to passionately follow her dad's advice to "love what you do!" Debbi is the founder, Chief Cookie Lover, and former chairman of Mrs. Fields Cookies. She has since sold her company and resides in Memphis, Tennessee, with her husband, Mike Rose, and family. Debbi is the mother of five daughters: Jessica (26), Jenessa (23), Jennifer (21), Ashley (17), and McKenzie (14).

Edward Martin Sivyer was a loving husband, father and loyal friend. He served his country proudly in World War II and worked for the U.S. Navy as a talented welder who resided in Oakland, California.

Karyn McLaughlin Frist

■ WILLIAM E. MCLAUGHLIN II

THE MAN IN THE MOON is my dad. On a clear night, when the moon is full, I love to walk to a dark spot and look into the heavens and see Daddy's face looking down at me. It seems like a childish thing to do, especially since my dad died when I was twenty-seven years old.

The memories of Daddy are numerous, so many I could fill a book! So many moments stick out in my mind. For instance, Daddy once gave my sister and me each a $2 bill numbered in consecutive numbers. He said, "Keep these forever and, if we ever get separated, we can know when we find each other by these $2 bills." I never felt lost from Daddy even when I went to college, as he wrote me every Monday. He signed his letters, "Love U, Daddy Boy." My roommates asked me, "So what did Daddy Boy have to say today?" I looked forward to those letters every week. I am so glad that I kept many of them.

Daddy's love for God, family, and his country was immense. In a letter he wrote to his mother dated August 11, 1945, from Germany, he said, "I heard the war is officially over, we're not sure so I had better run over to the Red Cross to the radio. We'll go to church if it's true and thank the Lord for saving so many lives." He closed by saying, "Now, Mother, don't worry about me any more, your wandering boy is coming home." His patriotism, due partly from his service in World War II, led him to wake us up every 4th of July blaring "Stars and Stripes Forever" on the record player. Each of us waving our own American flag, my sister and I would follow my mother and daddy out the front door to raise up the stars and stripes. The entire time we prayed that one of our neighbors would not drive by and see us marching in our pajamas. He continued this tradition until the year he died. He called and woke us up with the song, even after we were grown up and Bill and I married.

Valentine's Day was another special day in our home. Daddy didn't do the easy thing and send flowers. He bought each of his "little girls"—my mother, sister and me—a spring outfit. It was always a soft spring color like pink, green, or lavender that he had spent time picking out, just for us. He was proud of his girls.

Every Sunday we got into the car for church and Daddy said, "You girls look so pretty, but not as pretty as your mother." It used to kind of hurt my sister's feelings, but as she got older she realized what a great example of true love for one's spouse he showed us. Our parents were crazy about each other.

In addition to his wonderful relationship with my mother, I remember Daddy's immeasurable love and respect for his mother. He made the long drive to visit her long after she ceased to recognize him. He held her hand and gave her detailed updates about each member of the family.

The memory that I hold closest to my heart is from 1978 when I was the victim of a violent crime. He accompanied me to Detroit to identify a man that had attacked me while I was in a hotel room. After teaching school in Dallas, Texas, I had applied for a job with an airline, knowing full well that Daddy would never let me "backpack around Europe." I had to overnight in Detroit, and a former employee of the hotel had a pass key and broke into my room. I was lucky—I had a black eye and a sprained hand, but was fine. I remember calling my parents the next day. As a parent now, I cannot imagine how they felt waiting for me to return to Lubbock later that night. Daddy hugged me when I got off the airplane like he had never hugged me before. He asked Mother to sleep in my room that night. A few days later, he walked into my room and told me that the man who had attacked me had been caught. I had been asked to go and identify him. Daddy discussed the trip with me and said that I did not have to go. I did not have to press charges. I did not need to ever go back to Detroit. He then said that that would be the easy thing to do. The other option was that this man would probably strike again. There was no doubt in my mind to make the trip.

Daddy went with me. I will never forget him wringing his hands as we stood behind the one-way glass as seven young men filed into a room and stood against the wall. There was absolutely no doubt which one had attacked me. I pointed him out and Daddy quickly whisked me out of the courthouse. We went to dinner on top of a revolving restaurant and sat on the edge looking over the city. He placed something, I just don't remember what, on the stationary part of the floor and told me to get it when it rotated around. It was a special evening that I will never forget.

Even when I could have taken the easy way out, he encouraged me to do what was right even if painful and hard. As a parent, I am sure he was devastated, but I never felt it.

I have always felt Daddy's presence. I often think of his letters when I pick up the mail. I check numbers on $2 bills, and on a starry evening I often walk to a dark spot on the lawn and look at the full moon and say, "I love YOU, Daddy Boy."

■ ■ ■

Karyn McLaughlin Frist, a graduate of Texas Christian University and former special education teacher, was born in Lubbock, Texas. She is married to the United States Senate Majority Leader, Bill Frist, MD. They live in Nashville, Tennessee, and Washington, DC, and have three sons: Harrison, Jonathan, and Bryan.

William McLaughlin II, was born on December 11, 1923, in Ralls, Texas. He graduated from Southern Methodist University in 1948 with a degree in business. He served on the Finance Commission of Texas and was involved in banking and farming in West Texas for over forty years. He married Kathryn Louise Loving on June 2, 1947, and had two daughters, Karyn and Patricia McLaughlin Thomas. He died on April 8, 1982.

Lyn Glenn

■ JOHN GLENN

ONCE UPON A TIME, in a land far away and a time long ago, before speed records, space flights, and political campaigns, lived a young girl. She had auburn hair and freckles like her father's. He told her that if someone asked, "Where did you get all of those freckles, little girl?" she could reply, "It rained and I rusted." It was a special joke they shared.

The young girl dreamed of roller skating, of flying down the sidewalk just like her only and older brother, Dave, whom she adored. Their family moved many, many times and Dave was her most constant, and sometimes most irritating, companion.

Lyn received skates as a gift from her parents, wonderful skates that had a key and fit onto the bottom of her sneakers. They were silver with bright red straps and seemed just perfect. She knew, really believed, that these were the best skates that anyone had ever owned.

She knew to be careful, to fall onto the grass, and not to go out on the road, stay on the sidewalks, and not go too far from home. But even with all of the caution, one day she took a terrible tumble. She fell forward and rocks and dirt were scraped into each of her knees. It was awful and hurt so much. She went running home, crying all the way. Her mother and father looked at her bloody knees and her father took her to the bathroom to wash the dirt and debris from the wounds. He put iodine on the injuries, which made her knees hurt even more. To help take the pain away, her father blew and blew and blew on the wounds, but the pain was still very bad. He told her that he did not want her to experience such pain, but the medicine would help keep her knees from getting infected and it was very important to put the iodine on both knees. Then he smiled and said he had an idea that would help them

both. It would help Lyn because the pain would be less and it would help her father because he did not like to see her in such pain. He left the bathroom and came back with a fan! He thought the fan could blow even harder on her knees to help the pain go away when the iodine was applied . . . and it worked! It was a win-win solution for Lyn and her father, and after many days of cleaning the wounds and applying iodine in front of the fan, her father said her knees were healed and she went back to enjoying her wonderful skates. And, yes, she eventually learned to fly down the sidewalk, just like her big brother.

This is a true story from fifty years ago when my family lived in Patuxent River, Maryland, near the Naval Air Station where Dad was a test pilot. I share it because it reveals a few of my father's special qualities. We were a typical Marine Corps pilot's family. When I fell, Dad was patient and did not shame or punish me for falling. He looked at the situation and thought outside of the box to find a better solution. He was tenacious and, over the many days of recovery, he made sure that we took care of my knees every day.

These qualities have been a lifelong example for me: approach a situation with an open mind and heart, and try to see things in a new, fresh way, letting curiosity be my guide. There is no shame in pushing hard and falling, but it is very important to get up, try again, and keep living with energy and enthusiasm to be the best that I can be. When people we love are in pain or trouble, be present with them. Empathy can bring emotional pain, but it also deepens the experience of being a living, sentient being. Though one's life may be busy and demanding, it is important to take time to be with the people in our lives, and to help the less fortunate or weakest among us.

These qualities are also reflected in my father's public life. He has devoted his life to serving our country, first as a Marine pilot, then as a NASA astronaut, and finally as a United States Senator from Ohio. He believes that public service is an honorable calling. He is a humble man who believes we should not forget where we came from, and keeps a wrench on his desk to remind him that his father, my grandpa, was a plumber in a small Ohio town. (He has also given a wrench to my brother and me as a reminder of our heritage.) Dad knows that in a democracy we must reach out to those with fewer resources and that opportunity is not just for those "in the castle." He also stands by his commitments, believing that, when an individual or government makes a commitment, the honorable action is to keep that commitment and to not "cut and run."

When I think of my father I am aware of his great curiosity, patience, love, loyalty, compassion, tenacity, and humility. And I am very proud to be the daughter of John and Annie Glenn.

■ ■ ■

Lyn Glenn: Daughter, Sister, Niece, Aunt, Godmother, Friend, Artist.

John Glenn: Husband, Father, Marine, NASA Astronaut, U.S. Senator, Educator.

Glenna Goodacre

■ HOMER GLEN MAXEY

WHEN I WAS GROWING UP my hero was a builder, developer, civic leader, philanthropist, and World War II Navy veteran—my dad, Homer G. Maxey. As my love for art grew, he became one of my most important teachers, taking our family on trips to Europe to see the major museums, cathedrals, and architecture. He also encouraged me to take lessons from visiting and local art instructors. Homer's ambitions were not in the visual arts, but his creative juices flowed—building houses, hotels, and apartments.

Homer, his father, and his three brothers were all in some aspect of the construction business, developing Texas communities. At age nine or ten, I eagerly sorted hardware at Daddy's lumberyard in Lubbock, surrounded by the wonderful smell of wood. Perhaps that's where my own passion for creating was born. I learned much, too, from my mother, Melba Tatom Maxey, who was a talented decorator. After college I was painting portraits, raising two babies, and building a few houses myself.

I turned from painting to sculpture in 1969 and Daddy's interest and admiration grew. My first bronzes were small children and life-size portrait busts of West Texas characters—prominent Lubbock businessmen, Texas Tech professors, plus Texas historians—many of whom were his close friends. Homer was such an enthusiastic fan that I jokingly used to say that the "G" in his name stood for Glenna.

I will always be appreciative of my father's love for me and his respect for my talent. A lesson I learned directly from Homer was to aspire to the best, fulfill every potential, create better sculptures, and beat the competition. My parents attended every art opening and sculpture dedication, puffed with pride.

My career flourished. Concurrently, Homer's business grew into a multimillion dollar empire involving real estate, lumber, and cattle. Then, in a suspicious bank foreclosure, his assets were confiscated. A man of tremendous integrity, Homer was outraged and devastated, but he knew he had been the victim of illegal scheming and he fought back hard. Years of litigation followed. Daddy's David-and-Goliath battle with the bank is legendary in Texas legal history. He eventually settled his case, but ended up with only enough to barely cover his legal expenses. Despite everything during this terrible ordeal, he continued to express amazement at my work and to stay informed about my new pieces.

During his struggle, I couldn't help with his frustration and wounded pride, but the tables had turned and I was able to give financial support during Homer and Melba's last years. Daddy died in 1990, and Mother passed away in 1995. Sadly, neither of them were able to attend the unveiling in 1993 of my most rewarding work, the Vietnam Women's Memorial on the National Mall in Washington.

I often feel my parents' proud "presence" as I sign a monumental sculpture, receive an award, or strike a coin. I have prospered as a direct result of their early involvement and loving support of me and my art.

■ ■ ■

Sculptor *Glenna Goodacre* created the Vietnam Women's Memorial in Washington, the heroic bronze portrait of Ronald W. Reagan at the Reagan Library in California, and the obverse of the Sacagawea U.S. Dollar, among countless other public sculptures in America.

Homer Glen Maxey was a builder who played an important role in developing Texas after WWII. His landmark legal battle with a large banking firm occupies a significant place in the annals of Texas law.

Ruth Bell Graham

■ L. NELSON BELL

ONE OF THE GREATEST BLESSINGS of my life was the privilege of growing up in a godly and happy home. My parents—Dr. and Mrs. L. Nelson Bell—were medical missionaries in China (where my siblings and I were born), and in spite of their almost overwhelming schedules they always made sure our home was a loving and secure place.

Daddy loved baseball, and in his teens had been offered a contract to pitch for the Baltimore Orioles. He strongly felt, however, that God was calling him instead to study medicine and go to China as a missionary. He and Mother arrived in China in 1916, and only left when forced to do so by the outbreak of the Second World War.

Those were turbulent years in China's history, and our part of the country was often ravaged by civil unrest and banditry. I don't recall ever going to sleep at night without hearing gunshots in the countryside. Fortunately, they weren't after us, and I never saw Daddy or Mother show fear. They always believed they were in God's hands, regardless of the situation. When the Japanese took over our city (before Pearl Harbor), Daddy drove to the local Japanese headquarters and politely but emphatically made it clear that, although they now controlled the city, they had no authority over the hospital, since it was American owned. They respected him for his stand and never gave him any trouble.

Daddy's specialty was surgery, but, because the Chinese those days didn't trust "foreign devils" (as they called foreigners), most people came to the hospital only if they were in desperate condition. Daddy treated all who came with both skill and compassion—even bandits. On one occasion he treated a bandit with a severe head wound; the next day, when he drove into the city, there hanging over the gate was the bandit's head, with the bandages still on it!

Daddy and his staff encountered almost every medical problem imagina-

義
來

ble. I recall one woman with an abdominal tumor that was so large she had to carry it in a wheel barrow she pushed before her. When Daddy removed the tumor he found it weighed about ninety pounds. The poor woman only weighed ninety pounds herself, and once the tumor was removed she no longer could keep her balance and had to learn to walk all over again. As a result of his skill he was made a Fellow of the American College of Surgeons on his fortieth birthday—a high honor for a missionary surgeon.

Because of Daddy and Mother we children had an incredibly happy home life. Daddy had a great sense of humor, which the Chinese keenly appreciated, as did we children. He laughed a great deal, and entertained us with a constant stream of stories. Each day began with family prayers, including a hymn with Mother at the piano, followed by Daddy with a Scripture reading and prayer. This routine varied on Sunday mornings, with each of us allowed to choose a hymn from which we sang one verse. Sunday afternoons Daddy often went to the local prison to preach; we children had great fun telling people that Daddy spent his Sundays in jail. (He firmly believed people's souls needed healing as well as their bodies, and God could heal their souls through faith in Christ). Each Sunday evening we played Bible games, which not only taught us interesting Bible facts but were also fun. Above all, we learned the importance of living for Christ—not just from the Bible, but from our parents' examples.

That part of China is very hot in the summer, and many missionaries moved to the mountains to escape the heat. But Daddy and Mother found that packing and traveling in rural China with a growing family was too exhausting, so they endured the heat (and continued working). To compensate, Daddy had a swimming pool built in the side yard, a simple brick structure about ten by twenty feet and filled with water from the hospital's deep well. The water was so cold it caused condensation on the outside of a drinking glass, but it still gave us children countless hours of recreation.

On summer evenings we sat on the outside porch and sang songs, accompanied by Daddy on his guitar. As dark fell we loved to play hide and go seek, and Daddy frequently spoiled the whole game by using a flashlight to find us. On winter evenings, after Daddy had finished his hospital rounds, we sat around the fireplace while mother taught us handiwork and the men took turns reading to us—everything from Charles Dickens to Joel Chandler Harris. No matter how busy Daddy and Mother were, evenings were always family times.

After Daddy and Mother left China, he established a surgical practice in Asheville, North Carolina, and also became active in community and church affairs. The last year of his life he was elected moderator of his denomination, the Presbyterian Church in the United States. By this time Mother was an invalid, but Daddy always put her first and said that caring for her was the greatest privilege of his life. To make it easier on them I took supper to them in the evenings, and chuckled to find Daddy sometimes reading "Tugboat Annie" stories from the *Saturday Evening Post*.

China was always uppermost in his thoughts and prayers, however, and until the day he died in 1973 he prayed that he might be able to visit there again. Such was not to be, but shortly after the end of the Cultural Revolution the door unexpectedly opened for my brother, two sisters, and me to return to the city where Daddy and Mother had served so faithfully. One of our greatest joys was meeting people who not only remembered them, but told how their lives had been influenced by Daddy's service.

Some years after Daddy's death several Chinese doctors came to the United States. They made a special trip to visit Daddy's grave, out of respect for a man they had come to love and admire. On his tombstone they found the Chinese character for righteous, and on Mother's tombstone the Chinese character for come—both fitting symbols of their natures (see page 95). Interestingly, the character for righteous consists of the Chinese character for "lamb" superimposed on the character for "me." The character for come is composed of a cross with the image of a man on it, and the image of a man on the other side. Their exact origin is unknown, but they predate the arrival of missionaries to China. and speak eloquently of the message which motivated Daddy and Mother to devote their lives to serving the people of China.

■ ■ ■

Ruth Bell Graham, wife of Evangelist Billy Graham, was born at Qingjiang, Kiangsu, China, in June 1920. Mrs. Graham is the mother of five children, grandmother of nineteen, and great grandmother to a growing number.

Dr. L. Nelson Bell, and his wife Virginia served as medical missionaries in China from 1916 to 1941, where Dr. Bell was chief surgeon at the Presbyterian Hospital 300 miles north of Shanghai.

Jennifer Mulhern Granholm

■ VICTOR GRANHOLM

PARENTING SOUNDS SQUISHY. Dad wasn't squishy. Dad was a rock. I don't think the most enlightened, informed, in touch, and in tune New Age dad could have given me what my dad did. Our favorite meal was indicative of Dad: a plate with equal thirds of chopped-up hamburger, boiled-not-squishy peas, and rice. Canned peaches and milk made a perfect dessert.

Mom said "Spread your wings! You can be anything." She was wild, exuberant, expressive. But Dad always had his feet planted. He was my mooring point. I never heard him swear. Can't remember him raising his voice. Don't think he ever lied. True to his generation, he is to this day somewhat ineffable. He doesn't much talk about how as a young boy he understood his dad's premature death, or what it felt like for his brother Ron and him to work at the lumber mill to help support their family. Nor does he talk about what it was like for the solid son of stolid Swedes to move his young family from Vancouver to L.A. so he could work in a bank.

There's nothing flashy about Dad. He worked his way up the banking ladder, from his first days as a teller to the prime of his career when he could evaluate loans, businesses, real estate, and banks themselves. He never got a degree, but it was his work ethic that led me to both of mine. He taught me to do things right and do the right things. I was proud of him when, on a break from law school, he brought me along to a picnic for a Chinese bank that was one of his clients. Neither he nor I understood the intricate formalities of the tea ceremony, but I could see that they understood his humility, his patience, and his respect for them and their culture.

In a world that loves drama, Dad was unflappable. When I was five he sheltered me beneath his arm on our olive-green couch and read children's tales every night. When I was eight he played dominos for hours, speaking more with his kind blue eyes than with words. When I thought algebra was going to send me to the madhouse, and when I just could "not get" what he was trying to show me, he would simply and quietly try another way to explain it; I got it, because he knew I would get it and never lost faith in me.

On crazy days in a governor's office in a global world, I find a certain steadiness, and I know where it came from. I think fondly of the great couple of years, when we drove together to San Francisco every morning at 5 a.m. He went to the bank in the city. I went to college across the Bay. What a spectacular gift he gave me—a quiet ride, with a quiet man, in love with life, and thrilled to have a good job in a great country.

○ ■ ■ ■

Jennifer Mulhern Granholm was born in British Columbia, but moved with her family to the United States when she was four years old. A graduate of California at Berkley and Harvard Law School, Ms. Granholm ended a line of forty-six male governors in Michigan, when she was elected in 2002. Prior to her election as governor, she was Attorney General for four years. She is married and has three children.

Victor Granholm was born in Penny, British Columbia. He married Shirley Dowden in 1955. Mr. Granholm got his first job in banking in 1953 as a teller at Toronto Dominion Bank and continues to consult to banks from his home in the San Francisco area.

Amy Grant

■ BURTON PAINE GRANT

MY FATHER is a quiet man . . . a thoughtful man. He has a beautiful smile and laughter that comes easily. I am the youngest of his four daughters. That he never made me feel for a moment that he wanted sons instead of daughters says a lot for my dad. He has a grateful outlook on life, and seems to roll with the punches. You know, something beautiful about him is that, even if I wrack my brain, I cannot dredge up one memory of my father speaking ill of another person. I think that's rare.

I do not know very many details about my father's childhood, maybe because he was an only child, and has had no siblings to banter back and forth with about the past saying, "Remember when we did this or that. . . ." Maybe because his own father died unexpectedly when my dad was a teenager, I've missed hearing a grandfather's perspective, saying to his grand-daughters, "Now when your daddy was about your age I remember him do-ing just such a thing." Whatever the reasons, some things about my dad are a mystery to me.

What I do know is that he seems pretty comfortable being in the pres-ent moment, and he is never in a hurry. He takes life at his own pace, and he loves the people in his life the same way—slow and steady. He never gives the impression that he's looking over your shoulder to see if someone more interesting or more important is approaching.

As I parent my own children in a cultural climate where lives are over-extended and schedules are over booked, I'm reminded that the pattern of my parents' choices during my childhood brought order and security to my life. I'm encouraged by the impact of simple, repeated acts of caring, the steady dependable rhythms of family life taught to me by my mom and dad—eating dinner together as a family, going to church together, saying

goodnight, saying good morning, making time to celebrate simple pleasures in life and in each other's lives.

It's funny how history repeats itself. All of the things that I routinely enjoy with my children I first enjoyed with my father and mother. When I was a child my father took me night fishing on the bay bridge in Sarasota, Florida. Now I enjoy taking my kids fishing in the ponds of Williamson County, Tennessee.

When I broke my collarbone in the sixth grade, he taught me how to play ping pong left-handed. We played every night. Today, our ping pong table stays set up in the garage, and most weeks the table gets some action. My dad woke me up every morning, sometimes with a short but sweet back rub. When we were kids, he bought a safe old horse for us to keep in the back yard to ride. We didn't have a horse trailer, so he rode it several miles through the neighborhoods from the farm where he bought it to our house. He loved hobbies, building things like a transistor radio or a ham radio receiver. He loved Morse code. (Believe it or not, I still know my name .— — — —,— —.)

From my dad I've inherited several things of which I am certain (brown eyes, a passion for projects, and the love of solitude and music) and some things for which I hope (his optimism, his gentleness, and his ability to see the best in people).

My father is a quiet man, but his presence in my life has shaped me as surely as the Colorado River has shaped the canyons in the Western states. That imprint is timeless—like father, like daughter . . . steady as she goes.

■ ■ ■

Amy Grant has sold over 25 million albums, and has won six Grammy Awards® in her pop/gospel music career. She has achieved such breakthroughs as being the first contemporary Christian artist to have a platinum record, the first to hit #1 pop and the first to perform at the Grammys®.

Dr. *Burton Paine Grant*, a physician for over fifty years, is best known for his work as a radiation oncologist at the Sarah Cannon Cancer Center at Centennial Hospital in Nashville, Tennessee.

Patricia Hooks Gray

■ BENJAMIN LAWSON HOOKS

T HE REVEREND Benjamin Lawson Hooks is widely known as a minister, an orator, a civil rights advocate, an attorney, a judge, and a past executive director of the NAACP. However, in my eyes, he is simply Dad, the one who has influenced me in uncountable ways and who has left a profound effect on my outlook on life.

It has often been stated that "the best things you can give children next to good habits are good memories." If I could pen a book, it would be entitled, *Unvoiced Lessons Learned from My Dad*.

In our formative years, a lot is learned from the role models in the environment. I can remember my mom, Frances, and Dad wanting me to improve my secretarial skills by typing my dad's handwritten speeches. The problem was that I became so engrossed in the messages from the speeches that my typing didn't get better. However, my thirst for unknown facts did. The speeches were so enlightening that I acquired a vast amount of knowledge on varied topics and the wonder and power of God. To this day, I still don't enjoy typing on the computer but I love surfing the Internet websites, seeking and devouring information.

As a civil rights advocate, I knew that Dad was something special. I attended Fisk University in Nashville, Tennessee. One year I participated in a sit-in at Morrison's Cafeteria. My picture ended up in the paper. Both of my parents reminded me that I was sent to Fisk to get an education and to not let anything get in the way of that. From that experience I learned that parents are always protective of their children. This left me with a warm, fuzzy feeling. I am still protective of my grown sons, Carlos Jr. and Carlton.

Family is important to Dad. My sons initially thought that their papa lived on an airplane. However, when possible Dad and Mom were rushing from the airport to observe Carlos Jr. in a school play or to take them both to

NAACP conventions. A highlight for Dad was speaking at Carlton's high school graduation. I have never missed a Christmas with my parents. I still get a special feeling whenever my dad asks, "Patty-Pat, when are you coming home?" Dad is the "godfather" of a huge extended family. He is our advisor, protector, and comforter. He's always there with encouragement and uplifting words for everyone.

On a humorous note, when I was presented as a debutante, my mom insisted that Dad purchase a new tuxedo. The one he owned was a little tight and a bit frayed. However, Dad very unassumingly stated that he wasn't going to be on center stage; therefore, his suit was just fine. Needless to say, he was quite embarrassed when the dads had to walk the runway with their daughters in full spotlight. It was also noticeable the other dads were fashionably dressed in the latest tuxedo styles. From that point on my mom started shopping and buying everything for my dad, whether he needed it or not. Sometimes we have to listen to others; they just may know what they are talking about.

Dad is a dynamic scholar with a phenomenal photographic memory. He especially enjoys poetry. One of his favorites is "What Happens to a Dream Deferred" by Langston Hughes. I can discuss any topic with my dad and the experience leaves me with a wealth of new viewpoints on the issues. When writing units for one of my classes, I informed Dad and instantly he and my mom planned a trip so that I could gain new insights on the topics: the French Revolution, a trip to France to visit the Palace of Versailles, or the Industrial Revolution, a trip to London where it began.

My dad has been quite a positive inspiration in my life and I just want to thank him for the memories, for the lessons learned, and for enabling me to not have some of my dreams deferred.

■ ■ ■

Patricia Hooks Gray is a retired public school reading specialist. Presently, she is an adjunct professor at Xavier University in Cincinnati, Ohio.

Reverend Dr. Benjamin Lawson Hooks has worn various hats as a lawyer, judge, FCC Commissioner, past Executive Director of the NAACP, businessman, civil rights crusader, adjunct professor, and Supreme Chancellor and Grandmaster of different fraternal organizations. Currently, he is the pastor of the Greater Middle Baptist Church in Memphis, Tennessee.

Alexa Hampton

■ MARK HAMPTON

GIVEN THE FACT that I have carried on my father's decorating business, I'm sure that, if anyone ever wastes a minute thinking about it, they imagine my relationship to my father as simply that of an acolyte. During his lifetime, as an apprentice, I was probably perceived as trailing along in the wake of "The Great Man," taking notes on how to interview clients, measure for curtains or scale furniture, or (shudder!) how to fill out purchase orders. How far that all is from the truth!

I came to admire my father and eventually want to do what he did because he made everything in my childhood better with his ability to shape my world in such a different way from those of my friends. Everything my father did was informed by his artist's soul. His love of art, beauty, music, and style changed my life long before I understood how it played into the professional life that would serve to inspire my choice of career.

His style and wit and talent came out in the drawings he made for my sister and me at the drop of a hat, in the faces he painted on us for Halloween, in the rhyming songs he made up and sang to make long car rides go faster, in the cardboard ornaments he made for our Christmas trees and the eggs he painted for Easter and in the watercolor cards we received on Valentine's Day and for every birthday.

His art studios were everywhere. They might be on a crowded kitchen counter, in a garage where he painted birthday games and banners, or in the middle of three-across airplane seats where he kept us girls quiet and amused on long trips with drawings he turned into something fabulous from a scribbled line or two of ours. (Sitting across from us, blissfully taking a break in an aisle seat, our mother smiled gratefully.)

My father had a wonderful singing voice, had taught himself to read music and play the piano, and he loved to dance. We girls (my sister Kate and I) learned to dance in the time-honored fashion of standing on his feet, until it was time to be thrillingly dipped or twirled. Though he loved classical music perhaps best, he was always crazy about rock and roll and R&B and taught us not only to dance to it (some credit here for my mother, too), but to appreciate its genius. Stevie Wonder will always be the family favorite.

I was so proud of him when he came to school on Father's Day and all my friends clamored for him to draw something special for them—and he did. Even my art teacher could be caught asking for a sketch to keep for herself. He cut out elaborate paper dolls for us that were things of beauty, drew our portraits and, if asked, didn't hesitate to sit himself down at the piano and play us any song we wished.

By training, my father was an art historian with a masters from NYU's Institute of Fine Arts. He was given a Ford Foundation grant to study museum curatorship at the Metropolitan Museum of Art and MOMA and nearly became a curator himself. So, he made sure that his daughters were given a thorough knowledge of museums. This was easy at home, since we lived just a few blocks from the Met and the Guggenheim. Museums were also a big part of sightseeing wherever we went, from Chicago to Calcutta. Through my father's eyes, I was shown how to look at art, and, wisely, he never made us stay so long that we got tired of it. On trips, we looked at a specific work or two (notice brush strokes, composition, and the like), and then we returned later to see more. In addition to museums, he wanted his daughters to share in his love of houses, palaces, and gardens.

I was lucky enough to inherit a tiny bit of my father's drawing and painting ability, and, as I grew older, this—along with the experience of sharing his life and enthusiasms—inevitably led me to wanting to share in his work as well. There are many things that he taught me that have helped me succeed professionally. However, his most important lesson to me was not how to work, but how to live. He taught me to try to bring art, music, and beauty into every single day of my life in both profound and mundane ways.

■ ■ ■

Alexa Hampton is the president and featured designer of Mark Hampton, LLC. She appears regularly in the top 100 lists of such magazines as Architectural Digest. *In 2004, Alexa became a cast member of the PBS show* This Old House *and* Find! *In 2005, she was appointed designer of Trowbridge House, the official residence for former U.S. presidents in Washington, DC. She currently designs featured lines for Kravet Fabrics, Hickory Chair Co., and Stark Carpet.*

Mark Hampton was an internationally known interior decorator based in New York. He worked with Sister Parrish, David Hicks before founding the firm of Mark Hampton, Inc. His clients included the first President Bush and Ambassador Pamela Harriman, among others. In addition to countless private residences, his projects included the White House, Washington's Blair House, the City of New York's Gracie Mansion, and the American Academy in Rome. Today, his work is considered iconic and remains highly influential.

Susan Billington Harper

■ JAMES H. BILLINGTON

MY FATHER was never the type to putter around the house on weekends fixing things, mowing the lawn, or tending to garden beds. Instead, he usually worked in his study, surrounded by books and completely absorbed in a world of ideas. When my younger sister first learned from our mother that babies were made "when Daddy planted a seed in Mommy," she shot back, "That's IMPOSSIBLE. Daddy has never planted a single seed in his entire life!" The four Billington children regularly went to sleep at night to the staccato lullaby of our father's manual typewriter, so we were sure there was always a new book in gestation even if we didn't believe the part about the seeds.

Yet, with all this intellectual activity, my father was not remote or distant. He involved us in his intellectual life from the beginning and ignited interests that led us all to great universities and, in my case, to a career in scholarship. As a little girl, I was allowed to sit under the baby grand piano inside the living room while he led college precepts for Princeton students—all men back then—who spoke in long sentences laced with words like "intelligentsia." I was enlisted to number and renumber pages and footnotes of his book manuscripts and, eventually, to be a research assistant in major libraries in America and Europe. When I visited Yale as a prospective student with my father, we got no further than Sterling Library on the college tour because the card catalogue was simply too tempting. While the rest of the prospective students continued to the dining rooms, gym, and dorms with the guide, we stayed in the library looking up references for my father's books. When I enrolled as a student, I didn't know much about the college but I was an expert on the library!

My father also taught me the profound importance and joy of learning about other people and cultures. My first school was an outdoor park in

Helsinki, Finland, where my sister and I were entrusted each day, faces protected from frostbite with Vaseline, to a portly "Park Auntie." At the age of six and eight respectively, my sister and I were the first American students to attend "Special Polytechnic School #47" in Moscow, Russia, where we wore Soviet uniforms decorated with baby Lenin pins and made lifelong friendships with ordinary Russians. On the planes home from the sabbatical (no direct flights then), I was unable to understand why the stewardess would not respond to my repeated requests for water until I realized that I was speaking in Russian rather than in English.

My father had completed his doctorate in Russian studies while a Rhodes Scholar at Oxford at the beginning of the Cold War. His subsequent career was devoted to helping Americans understand their greatest and most dangerous adversary. Toward the end of the Cold War, I was given a similar opportunity to go to Oxford on a Rhodes Scholarship, where I completed a masters degree in philosophy, politics and economics and a doctorate in South Asian studies. This education is now enabling me, in a much more modest way, to help some Americans better understand new challenges and opportunities emerging from developing nations in a multi-polar world.

Being part of the first-ever "father-daughter" Rhodes team would never have been possible had my father and mother not infused our lives with a passion for learning and ideas. I don't remember them ever discussing our grades, but I do remember long conversations about the subjects we were studying. I remember visits to our home of great scholars and poets and I remember that the bookshelf seemed the most exciting place in the world to be. When I felt insecure, my father used to encourage me by saying, "Susan, you're going to become the first woman president of the United States!" His confidence gave me confidence to do things I would never have thought possible. But, even more importantly, his unconditional love gave me the assurance that, even if I never achieved worldly success, his love would always remain intact. My sister remembers pretending to fall asleep one night and hearing our father pray aloud for her. She never forgot the earnest and loving tone of this prayer, which he thought only God had heard. We never doubted that, in everything, our father relied entirely on his Father in Heaven. His faith in God permeated his life and, so also, ours. In the end, this has been the most important thing of all.

■ ■ ■

Susan Billington Harper, an independent writer and mother of four children, received her B.A. from Yale and her M.A. and D.Phil. from Oxford, taught writing and history at Harvard, and has served as Program Officer for Religious Scholarship at the Pew Charitable Trusts and Executive Director of the Templeton Prize for Progress in Religion.

James H. Billington, the thirteenth Librarian of Congress, received his B.A. from Princeton and his D.Phil. from Oxford, taught history at Harvard and Princeton, and served as director of the Woodrow Wilson International Center for Scholars before being appointed to his current position in 1987. Susan and her father were the first-ever father and daughter both to receive Rhodes Scholarships.

Leigh Ann Hester

■ JERRY DWAYNE HESTER

I'M A SERGEANT in the 617th Military Police Company of the Kentucky National Guard. I've been to Iraq, and been in the middle of firefights in which I defended convoys against Iraqi insurgents. Because of one of those fights, I became the first woman ever to win the Silver Star for combat. But behind the soldier, under the fatigues, I am, and have always been, my dad's little girl.

My dad is a good ol' country boy who will talk your ear off if you let him! Whether you are an eighty-year-old woman or a ten-year-old boy, my dad will strike up a conversation with you and will take a genuine interest in what you have to say. We've been in stores and my mom and I will tell him that we need to go and he'll just keep chatting for about twenty more minutes. I get embarrassed sometimes, but I really love that quality about him.

I am the younger of two girls. My sister has always been more of a mama's girl, and me, well, I guess you could say that I'm kind of the son that my dad never had. When I think about our relationship, I'm always reminded of a picture of me and my dad under his old car, Dad teaching me how to change the oil. If my dad had had his way, he would have taken me everywhere with him—including to work! I have so many great memories of time spent fishing, hunting, going to ball games together.

One fishing story stands out in my memory and still comes up every now and then because of the huge "fish" that I caught. When I was about twelve years old, we went bass fishing in Georgia with my next-door neighbor and his daughter, who was a little younger than me. Well, four people in a bass boat is about two too many, as the casting can get a little tricky—and dangerous—especially with two young girls in the boat. At one point, I went to cast my line and, when I yanked it forward to let it go, it snagged on something. I remember looking back as this all happened and saw my dad's hat fly off his head! I thought that the line had gotten caught on the hat, but the expression of shock on my dad's face was all I had to see to realize what had happened. The bait—a Rapala minnow with two three-pronged hooks attached to the line—had hooked itself in the back of my dad's head! Needless to say, we cut that fishing trip short and ended it with a little trip to the emergency room. My dad, with his great sense of humor, still makes the occasional joke about how I caught the biggest "fish" in Georgia!

Our great relationship continued into middle school when my dad took me to see the high school boys play basketball. He thought that I would become a better player by watching the boys play ball. I truly think that going to those games really helped me as an athlete and a competitor later in high school when I played softball and basketball. My dad is a very wise man—when I fail, he tells me how to be better; when I succeed, he tells me just how proud he is of me.

Even though I enjoyed basketball, softball, hunting, and fishing, I've wanted to be a soldier for as long as I can remember. My parents don't have a military background, but, with an uncle who fought in Vietnam and a grandfather who fought in World War II, I got the itch early on to join the military. My mom and dad have always trusted my judgment and supported my decision 110 percent to join the Kentucky National Guard.

When I was deployed to Iraq, my parents were obviously very worried for my safety, but knew that I had a very important job to do. While in Iraq I was fortunate enough to get to call home. I didn't get to talk to my dad a lot because he was at work when I called, but every time that I did get to talk to him he always ended the calls with "Take care of #1." I felt a great sense of security when I heard his voice. It was as if he were right there with me and we were in a boat together, waiting for the next big fish to come along.

■ ■ ■

Leigh Ann Hester was born in Bowling Green, Kentucky, on January 12, 1982. She was deployed on October 5, 2004, with the 617th Military Police Company (Kentucky National Guard) in support of Operation Iraqi Freedom 3 and became the first female to receive the Silver Star for combat action.

Jerry Dwayne Hester was born on January 30, 1954, in Indianapolis, Indiana. He currently works as a maintenance technician for Renaissance Mark and resides in Bowling Green, Kentucky, where his daughter grew up.

E. D. Hill

■ WILLIAM "W. H." TARBOX

MY FATHER was born wealthy, which stands in shocking contrast to what you'd think if you ever met him. When he passed away in 1999, the car he drove was a used VW. While he had some very nice clothes, you would usually find him wearing an old cashmere sweater with patches on the sleeves. And after his death it was just as common for me to have a truck driver tell me how much he was missed as it was to hear it from a businessman.

The reason my father was so widely liked and admired was because he had perfected the art of humility and graciousness. It is a gift he tried to pass on to me.

Dad went out of his way to build up others. I first realized it when I was about ten. If someone complimented my father on, say, a new car, my father highlighted its shortcomings, turned the compliment around, and by the end of the chat the person driving the economy car felt he was lucky not to have a luxury sedan. My dad stressed that I should never let my good fortune make others feel uncomfortable or less significant.

Dad always looked for and found the good in people. That is what he focused on. When speaking to others, he always made them feel intelligent and significant. By treating others with respect, he was always regarded with respect in return. By not speaking ill of others, he was never spoken ill of. He was always the first to extend a helping hand. My dad taught me that the good that I passed on to others would be remembered, returned, and would make life better for everyone.

Dad was never showy. If he were going to an event with people of lesser means, he always drove an old car and dressed in a way to blend in. When someone asked what we had done over vacation, my dad talked about the projects around the house he'd gotten to in the last half instead of the skiing trip to Europe in the first half. My dad taught me never to talk about my possessions and, if pressed, to be understated.

Dad bought what he needed and used what he bought. Remember that new car? We kept it for twelve years. When buying clothes, my dad stressed buying the highest quality because it had the greatest durability. And regardless of what the item was, it was always taken care of.

I'm not sure if it was as difficult then as it seems to be now to instill those lessons. Children want the latest electronic gadgets, chicest clothing, and most expensive sneakers, not because they are a good value but simply because they are new. "McMansions" are built for families of four. I'm still trying to figure out how four people can find each other in a 15,000-square-foot house! Sweet sixteen parties and bar mitzvahs look like Broadway productions because parents want their child to "remember it their whole lives," as if they'd forget the day they turned sixteen if they had a small celebration.

I don't have the biggest house, the newest car, or a new wardrobe. What I have is contentment. I am comfortable in my life and I am happy for the success of others. My father couldn't have given me a more valuable gift.

■ ■ ■

E. D. Hill is an Emmy-winning reporter who hosts Fox and Friends *which is seen in seventy-one countries on the Fox News Channel. She has five children and three step-children.*

William "W. H." Tarbox, was an aeronautical engineer who worked for TWA for twenty years. He, like his daughter, had a passion for fishing and the outdoors and was active in numerous philanthropies.

121

Kay Bailey Hutchison

■ ALLAN BAILEY

M Y DAD WAS ONE of our small Texas town's leaders and most beloved citizens. When I think of the mainstay of America, good people who ask for nothing from government and feel they should give back to our country for the blessings we have, I think of my dad.

He was a small businessman. In the mid-1930s, he read in the _Galveston Daily News_ that Union Carbide was building a refinery in nearby Texas City. So, he moved to an area close by, bought land, and started developing subdivisions to provide homes for the people who would soon move to the area.

He helped build La Marque into a family-oriented place with quality public schools. He cofounded the Rotary Club to assure community involvement by the business leaders.

He loved young people. He attended all the high school football games before, during, and after any of his children were there. He donated the school book covers for all the schools every year.

Through the years, he was urged to run for mayor, but he never would run for public office. He did, however, believe it was a civic duty to support the political system—sending $25 a year to both the Republican and Democratic parties.

I recently heard a story from a retired NASA engineer. He said he bought a used car from my dad. When he told Dad he was working on his PhD, Dad told him he wouldn't take any payment until the young man had finished his PhD—not even a down payment. Four years later, the young PhD started paying Dad for the car.

He did not believe in frills. Though many of our college friends had cars, we never did. When I started law school, and it was necessary for me to drive to campus, rather than walk, my aunt gave me her ten-year-old clunker that she was about to "trade in." She believed in running a car until it was ready for

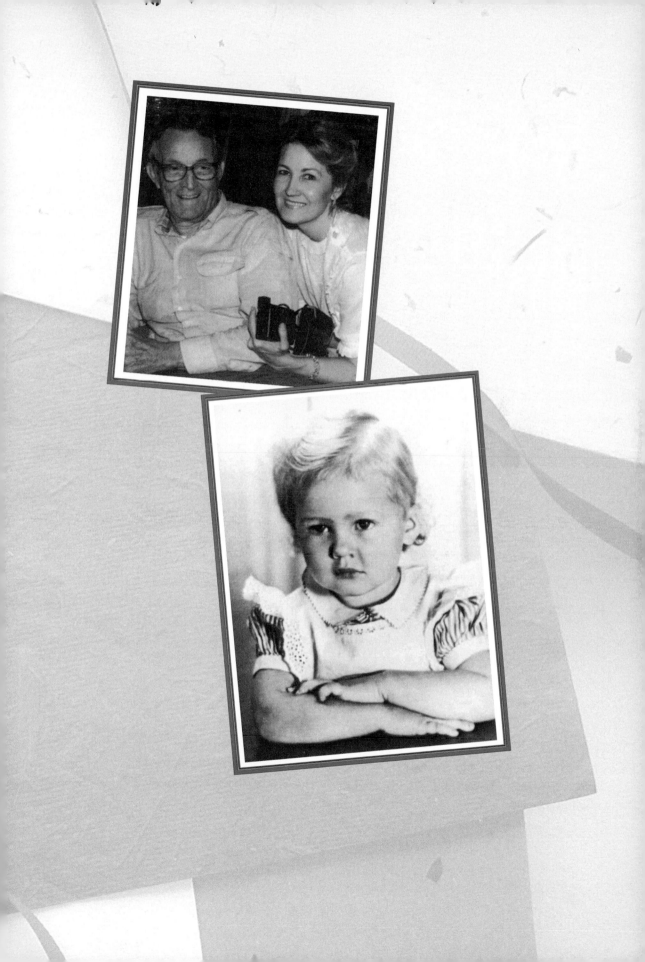

the junkyard. So, while most of my friends had better stock, it was adequate for my purposes . . . though I must admit few of my friends asked me for a ride!

When my brother was in undergraduate school, he faced the same car ban. But being five years younger than me, and bolder, he asked my dad, directly, if we couldn't have a car because we were poor. To which my dad said, "No, I could buy you a car . . . but I won't . . . because it just wouldn't be right."

Dad's generosity when it "was right" was boundless. The family car was always a Plymouth or a plain Buick. I never remember anything else—except once. My mom was diagnosed with cancer in 1960. She was told it was rapidly growing and could claim her life in six months. She took strong chemotherapy to try to stop the spread and then had surgery at M.D. Anderson in Houston. During the chemo, Dad was trading in her car, because it was time for a new one. She told him please not to do it, as there might not be a need for another car the next year. Mother came home a few days later to find a brand new Cadillac in the driveway—his way of saying "you are going to live and I love you very much!" Mom's surgery was successful. She lived to the age of 86 (and back to Buicks).

When he was in his last days, I was sitting with him in the hospital. I asked him what were his happiest times. He said without hesitation, "When I knew I had enough saved to send all three of you to college." There was never a question that we would go to college. And when I told Dad I wanted to go to law school, he didn't blink. He said he thought it was great and encouraged me, though it was very unusual for women at the time (there were thirteen women in our class of 500).

When I think of my formative years, I so appreciate my experience. I loved growing up in our small town and having the support of my parents through good times and bad. I am lucky to have had a role model who was honest, good, and decent. It seemed normal and stable; a perfect foundation with which to meet the ups and downs of today's fast-moving world.

I have never been able to talk about my dad in public speeches—when I would so like to pay tribute to him and my mother for all of the opportunity they gave to me. However, I always get a catch in my throat and fear I would not be able to get through it, so I avoid mentioning the sturdy base of support they provided in my life.

Kay Bailey Hutchison is the first woman elected to the U.S. Senate from Texas.

Allan Bailey, helped settle and incorporate their hometown, La Marque, Texas.

Billie Jean Moffitt King

■ BILL MOFFITT

I**T'S AN UNWRITTEN RULE** somewhere that says there is a special bond between fathers and their daughters. It's definitely true with me and my dad.

My dad, Bill Moffitt, in his day was an all-around jock. He was really good at several sports and, while basketball was his favorite, he also excelled at track and field and had a true connection with baseball. He even spent a short stint as a major league scout.

If you met us today you would see that a good part of my personality—especially my competitive nature—comes from Dad. My mother named me after him—mostly because I was born while he was away serving in World War II. Actually, he never saw me until I was two years old, when he returned home from the war.

After the war Dad did several things, and he eventually ended up as a firefighter with the Long Beach Fire Department. He drove the fire truck and had the respect of everyone at the firehouse. They all trusted that Dad would get them to the fire in the shortest amount of time and they respected his judgment. He had found his true passion, and it was a career that he loved and it treated him well.

During his days at the firehouse, Dad always worked out. You have to put this in perspective because, in the 1950s, lifting weights, running, and being committed to staying in shape just weren't the norm . . . unless you lived in Bill Moffitt's house in Long Beach.

Dad's schedule allowed him to be home every other day, and I have great memories of us always playing catch, shooting baskets, or doing some type of physical activity. My younger brother Randy (who went on to pitch for the Giants, Astros, and Blue Jays) and I were always pushed to be active, and Dad wanted to make sure we had access to coaches and programs that helped us improve. His interest in our physical future didn't really seem like a big deal at the time, and it probably wasn't until we were both much older that we truly recognized the impact of those simple, supportive moments on our professional careers and lives.

As I started to play more tennis in my junior years, Dad was always there to show me the big picture and help me keep things in perspective. That guidance helped me well into my career. Once, when I had not shown the best sportsmanship on the court, we went home after the match and Dad took me into the garage, where he fired up his electric saw and started to cut my racquet in half. He wasn't always the greatest sport himself, so I thought it was funny. But, you know that little trick has always stuck with me.

My dad was, and still is, a very competitive man. I once saw him play a pick-up basketball game at age forty-two and let's just say he was intense. He is in his eighties now, and he and Mom still tear up the swing dance floor every Thursday night at the Pine Cone Supper Club in Arizona.

I have always been proud of Mom for naming me after my dad. People have always told me the name fits me well and I am really happy being Billie Jean Moffitt King.

■ ■ ■

Billie Jean Moffitt King was named one of the "100 Most Important Americans of the 20th Century" by Life Magazine.

Bill Moffitt was a long-time firefighter in Long Beach, California. He has since retired to Arizona where, along with Billie Jean's mother, Betty, he continues to be an inspiration to Billie Jean, her brother Randy, and their extended families.

Hadassah F. Lieberman

■ SAMUEL FREILICH

MY FATHER taught me so very much. His strengths empowered me. His expectations nourished my growth through the good times and sustained my strength in bad times.

Daddy's ability to grapple with the historical realities that were thrust upon him taught me that we need tools and vision and direction to survive difficult times and that, most of all, we have to believe in ourselves.

As children we sometimes try to imagine our parents at younger ages, before they even knew that we would exist. Photographs give us a glimpse of those earlier times, and family members and friends often share their vignettes and jokes to flesh out imaginative reflections of "Daddy." What was he like when he was younger? Did he play with his friends in that park? Where was his house?

What a contrast it is to try to imagine a past when nearly everything was marked for destruction. Few if any relatives remain; occasionally a neighbor or community member or colleague is discovered, often living in another country or distant city. Miraculously, some photographs and memoir pieces appear, providing you with very little with which to piece your history together. Later oral histories might be recorded on tape recorders, but as a child you think "Who will want to listen?" Early on I realized that my father was not only a survivor, but an immigrant forced to adapt to a new language, home, and culture. As he wrote in his memoirs: "I left Prague in the spring of 1948 with my wife of one year, Ella, a survivor of Auschwitz, and our infant daughter, Hadassah. We settled briefly in New York City where I took on the task at age forty-five of learning my sixth language."

I still recall returning home to my parents after my first day in kindergarten when I announced that I would no longer speak "Yiddish, only English." I explained that otherwise I would not make friends. My memories of

Daddy in those years were of the hours he spent over his tape recorder laboriously repeating sentences over and over, so as to try to lose an accent for a more "New England" English.

Adjusting to a totally new way of life had its daily challenges. The European schedule of long strolls was recreated in our daily family walks around a reservoir at the top of our street in Gardner, Massachusetts. My brother and I ran and jumped around the conversations on current events or historical commentary. Friday night and Saturday was the time for the Jewish Sabbath and Sunday was always family time for walks, picnics, or road excursions in our car. Other adjustments included my parents' acknowledgement that perhaps our picnic baskets packed for every excursion might require the purchase of a 7-UP in response to my dear little American brother's screams. My parents forgot their frugality and gave in to him.

Squandering time was not appreciated. My hours of playing with a "BetsyWetsy" doll were greeted by my father's question, "How can you waste so much time with a doll whose sole function is to wet her pants?"

Dinners were a time for heated debates about current or historic events. Discussions of politics, history, and controversial newspaper articles led to exchanges which prepared me to join forensic debating leagues. By the time I rose from the table, my throat was often hoarse from making my points to a father who did not waver in his opinion despite my "brilliant" arguments. Later, I would digest his opinions and find myself concurring on some points.

I understood at an early age how my parents saw my brother and me as the proof and purpose of their survival. How often I overheard the Yiddish phrases expressed in undertones, how my brother and I were their "jewels," the "apple of their eyes," and the "stars in the sky."

The biggest gift that my father gave me as his daughter is that he was a role model for strength and adaptation, skills that are needed to face the new realities that are a constant presence in our lives.

■ ■ ■

Hadassah F. Lieberman was born in Prague, the child of Holocaust survivors. She is married to Senator Joseph Lieberman.

Rabbi Samuel Fredich immigrated from Czechoslovakia to the United States in 1949, together with his wife and infant daughter, shortly after the Communist takeover.

Nancy Lopez

■ DOMINGO LOPEZ

MY DAD OWNED an auto body-repair shop where I spent many afternoons washing windows and helping out in any way I could. He was a man of integrity, and I saw this trait in the way that he was with the people who came into the shop. If someone wasn't happy with the way that something looked, if the paint job wasn't coming out just right, Dad would redo it. He truly believed in "doing things right and doing what you say you are going to do." I think that by osmosis I took these lessons to heart and have applied them to everything I have done in my life.

In his free time, Dad was a pretty good amateur golfer. I remember sunny days spent at the golf course, watching Mom and Dad hit balls and enjoying being with them in such a wonderful setting. Eventually my dad put a golf club in my hand and told me, "Every time you swing at it, hit it"—very simple advice, but words that have stuck with me throughout my life and career as a player on the LPGA tour.

At one point, my dad realized that I had some talent and with practice could become a good golfer. So that's what I did—I practiced. We spent all of our time on the golf course. Dad got someone to watch the shop and he took me to the golf course as much as possible. We even drove a couple hours away to Albuquerque where my parents had friends who belonged to the Albuquerque Country Club, a club with a more challenging course than the one that I was used to. When I wasn't actually on the course, I still practiced. My dad dug a hole in our backyard so that I could practice my trap shots. I remember him saying, "I'm gonna dig a hole in the ground so you can practice, 'cause you stink."

I spent most of my childhood on the golf course and when I got to high school encountered some obstacles because I was a girl and there was no women's golf team. Wanting me to practice as much as I could, my dad supported me in my desire to be a part of the men's team, believing that by playing with boys, who were much better than I was, I would become a better golfer.

More than anything else, my dad was my "mental mentor." My only teacher until about five or six years ago, Dad was extremely positive and loving in his coaching. While other coaches lectured and made their players afraid of losing, my dad never made me fear failure. In fact, he was the most tender when I was playing badly. He always gave me a hug and said, "It's ok, honey. You're not perfect. Let's work a little harder." The one and only time I succumbed to a temper tantrum of sorts, throwing my golf club out of frustration, my dad informed me that he would not ever allow me to be one of "those" players. I never felt pressure from him. I remember toward the end of my career I said that it was time to slow down, and he replied, "You're right, you've done everything you can do."

I received my LPGA tour card after my sophomore year at the University of Tulsa. Shortly thereafter, my mother passed away. It was a difficult time for both my father and me and we were a support system for each other as I began my journey in the LPGA. After all of the countless hours my dad worked, saving money to pay for the expensive green fees and trips to countless tournaments, I was so happy to be able to say "thank you" by taking him with me on the Concorde and to countries such as England and Australia. He was just happy to be with me.

Dad was hysterical and everyone had a story about him. He was not only dear to me, my sister, and my daughters, but was loved by everyone who met him. Women of all ages loved Dad, and I have to admit that he liked to flirt! I remember one time I was playing in the Jamie Farr Classic in Toledo. Because Dad was getting older and could no longer walk the entire course, I rented him a handicap cart. He might have been slow on foot, but he sure was a little speed demon when he got behind the wheel of that cart! On this particular day, I was just about to tee off on the 18th hole. I guess Dad had worn out the cart, because, as I glanced back, a group of five women were struggling to push the cute little man up the hill as they laughed, while he entertained them with his "classic" comments.

This laughter was a constant in Dad's life. When he passed away, the funeral home was filled with laughter—everyone who met him had a funny story. His down-to-earth, positive nature was contagious, and was a trait that stayed with him always. When he was seventy-nine, he became ill and his doctors told us that he had only six months to live. He ended up living for eight more years. We never told him about the six months and instructed his doctors to do the same. Dad was simply too positive and wouldn't have wanted to hear it. He was an incredible person, and, although he is gone, he is still a strong presence and "mental mentor" in my life.

■ ■ ■

Nancy Lopez lives in Albany, Georgia, with 1986 MVP ballplayer Ray Knight. She has three daughters—Ashley (22), attending Auburn University, Erin (19), attending Auburn University, and Torri (14), still at home. Even though Nancy won forty-eight times on the LPGA tour she feels her greatest accomplishments are her three wonderful daughters.

Domingo Lopez was always the light in Nancy's eyes. He passed away in Roswell, New Mexico, in 2002 from congestive heart failure. She will miss him dearly.

Anne Graham Lotz

■ BILLY GRAHAM

A WEEK AFTER my seventeenth birthday, I wrecked my mother's Volkswagen on the way to my high school baccalaureate, where my father, Billy Graham, was to present the message. Driving too fast, I collided with a huge Buick driven by our family friend, Mrs. Pickering. Her car was unhurt, but the side of Mother's little beetle was smashed in.

My mother's car was dented but still drivable, so I begged Mrs. Pickering not to tell my parents and then hurried on to the service. Just as I got to town, a police officer stopped me. "I can't believe this!" I fumed.

The policeman walked up to my window and said, "Well, little lady, it looks like you've been in a wreck." Without a word, I burst into tears. He warned me to "be more careful next time" and let me go.

I finally made it to baccalaureate and squirmed uncomfortably when my father stepped into the pulpit and looked straight at me. He told the audience what a wonderful daughter I was, how I had never caused him and Mother any problems, and what a joy I was to them. Listening to his words and remembering Mother's smashed-up VW in the parking lot, I prayed I would die!

Although I tried to bolt as soon as the service ended, somebody called me. "Anne, your father wants to see you."

Here it comes, I told myself, wondering how he had heard about my fender bender.

I found him outside in front of some news people waiting to take a picture of us on this special day. (Seeing the photo the next day on the front page of the *Asheville Citizen Times*, readers probably thought the mascara streaks on my face were due to all the happy emotions on that momentous occasion.)

Later, I drove slowly home, praying as I went, "Dear God, please let my

daddy be anywhere else—on the phone, in the study, taking a walk—just don't let him be anywhere I have to see him right now."

I parked the car so the bashed-in side was away from the house, silently slipped inside, and had started up the stairs when I felt a presence behind me. I turned to find Daddy standing there; his famous blue eyes pierced right through me.

He let me blubber on for awhile, then Daddy said four things that taught me a life's lesson, not only about my relationship with him, but about my relationship with my heavenly Father too. He said:

"Anne, I knew all along about your wreck. Mrs. Pickering told me. I was just waiting for you to tell me.

"I love you.

"We can fix the car.

"You're going to be a better driver because of this."

At that moment I realized what an incredibly wonderful father I had.

Sometime in your life, you're going to be involved in a wreck of some kind—a mistake in which you or a loved one gets hurt. Maybe you've done something to wreck your marriage or your health or your reputation or your relationship with a friend. You may think you can keep the thing you've done a secret from God. Or you may believe that what you've done is so awful He will turn His back on you. When that happens, don't hide from Him. Run to Him! Remember what He promised you in His Word: He knows all about you, and He will always love you, despite the mistakes you've made. Tell Him what you've done, and He will take your smashed-up life and put it back together again so that it's better than it was before. Then you will discover by experience what an incredibly wonderful heavenly Father you have!

■ ■ ■

Anne Graham Lotz, daughter of evangelist Billy Graham, is president and CEO of AnGeL Ministries. Anne has followed in her father's footsteps, sharing the Good News of Jesus Christ throughout the world through her books and spoken messages.

Dr. Billy Graham has preached the Gospel to over 210 million people in more than 185 countries. As a result, hundreds of thousands of individuals have made decisions to claim Jesus Christ as their Savior and Lord, thus fulfilling his personal goal—"My one purpose in life is to help people find a personal relationship with God, which, I believe, comes through knowing Christ."

Bonnie McElveen-Hunter

■ JOHN T. MCELVEEN

IT WAS NEARLY one o'clock in the afternoon on the Clemson University campus on December 7, 1941, but 6,000 miles away it was still early morning when a wave of Japanese torpedo planes swept in low over Pearl Harbor and began its deadly work.

As the news came crackling over the radio at Clemson, my father was just three months into his college career. There was, however, no hesitation about what he would do next: for him, the "date which will live in infamy" became the first day of a life that would take him from the firestorms of a world at war to the thin rim of the Earth's upper atmosphere and back.

My father was born on February 14, St. Valentine's Day, 1924, in the little town of Salley, between the tea-steeped headwater forks of the Edisto. My great-grandfather, Dr. Thomas R. McElveen, attended his birth and always hoped my father would follow him in a career in medicine.

The Lord had other plans. My father's first experience in the air came at the age of eight, when he took a ride in a JN-4D Jenny. It was a biplane that could be described as rugged at best. During the flight, the motor fell off. But the excitement of an emergency landing only fueled his enthusiasm.

After flying many missions in World War II, he received his college degree in mechanical engineering from Clemson and married my mother, then Madeline Bonneau Brown. By the 1950s, his career as an engineer was put on hold—he was called back to work with the planes he so loved. This passion led to my father's "call to service" as one of the original seven U-2 pilots in American history.

When I think of my dad, I think of a life filled with deep devotion and a sense of purpose. I think of a man willing to put service truly before self with an unyielding commitment to freedom, family, faith, and country.

That commitment took him away from his family and from me for long

periods of time. Yet every difficult goodbye was met with a celebrated and much-anticipated hello.

I cherished those homecomings. I can still feel my father's arms around me as he lifted me up in his sturdy, secure hug, with the first question: "What have you learned while I was gone?" My father always encouraged me to reach high in pursuit of knowledge and noble causes. He lived that leadership through his personal example.

No matter where he was in the world, my father never forgot my birthday and always sent beautiful yellow roses. To this day, yellow roses remind me of my loving dad.

He was a man of few words. A handsome man. A man who loved nature—planting things, nurturing them, watching them grow. It was true both in his garden, and in my life. He could never understand why anyone would sow anything simply or carelessly. There was always a sense of mission, even in his planting.

But most of all, I remember my dad's quiet assurance, and his deep love of me and our family. Although my dad is in the Lord's loving arms, I feel his presence with me every day as he is forever "my hero."

■ ■ ■

Bonnie McElveen-Hunter is the former U.S. Ambassador to Finland (2001–2003) and the CEO and owner of Pace Communications, Inc., the largest private custom publishing company in the United States. She currently serves as the Chairman of the American Red Cross.

John T. McElveen was one of the original seven U-2 pilots in World War II. He passed away just before Christmas 1996, at the age of seventy-two.

TOM MLECZKO

MY FATHER has taught me many things throughout my life, but most significantly he has taught me about the importance of enthusiasm. Whether it was teaching in his classroom, coaching football, hockey, or lacrosse, or simply being around others, he has always shown so much joy. Nowhere has this been more evident than in his career as a charter-fishing captain on Nantucket Island. He has fished Nantucket waters for almost forty years, and yet every fish he catches, or even sees someone else catch, seems as if it is the first fish he has ever seen. This trait, together with his uncanny knack for finding fish, has made him the best charter captain on the island.

Although I often went out on my dad's boat, the *Priscilla J.*, it was not until high school that I worked for him as a first mate, or "striker." He was a schoolteacher at our elementary school in the non-summer months so we would see plenty of him then, but the summer was an incredibly busy time for him, being on the water before sunrise and often staying out after sunset. I loved being out fishing on his boat, but I also loved being with my dad to watch him share his joy and love of fishing with others. This is his occupation, something he does day in and day out, yet even by Labor Day, he still gets giddy, eagerly rubbing his hands together when someone catches a fish, no matter how big or small the fish or the fisherman is.

Nantucket is known for catering to the powerful, wealthy, and famous during the peak summer months. Many of the people that fall into this category have fished and continue to fish with my dad. To him, however, anyone who steps on his boat represents the same thing: a love of fishing. He brings his passion to every charter, no matter who his guests are that day. Some of these people are accustomed to being the most influential person in their lives, yet when they are on the *Priscilla J.* it is my father who becomes the most powerful, the most famous, and the one whom they seek out for his extensive expertise. Whether it is the head of a major media network, that year's Cy Young Award winner, a former president of the United States, or the neighbor from down the street, they all get the same enthusiasm and joy from Captain Tom.

I owe so much of my success as a hockey player to what I have learned from my father. The passion he shows in his daily life has taught me to always love what I am doing. In loving my pursuits, I learned the value of working hard and enjoying the benefits that sacrifice and dedication bring. My parents have a pillow embroidered with this saying: "Do what you love, love what you do, and you will never work another day in your life." It is this mantra that my dad embodies and he has enriched so many lives by doing so.

■ ■ ■

In 1998, *A. J. Mleczko and her teammates made history by winning the first ever Olympic gold medal awarded in women's ice hockey; she also went on to win a silver medal in 2002 in Salt Lake City.*

Tom Mleczko has run his fishing business, "Captain Tom's Charters," for over forty years on Nantucket Island.

Anne Mulcahy

■ THOMAS DOLAN

SHORTLY AFTER I was named Chief Executive Officer of Xerox, I bumped into an old family friend who had been close to my father. We chatted for a few minutes and, as we parted, he said: "You know, Anne, it's such a shame your father wasn't alive to see your success. He would have been very proud."

Something about that comment unsettled me. It had the ring of truth, but it just didn't seem quite right. During the next few days, it kept coming back to me, causing me to reflect on my father and all he has meant to me. Would he, in fact, be proud of my business success?

An editor and writer, Dad was the epitome of creativity, principles, and values like fairness. He was ahead of his time on issues such as diversity and feminism. Years before it became politically correct, our home was filled with people of varying races, ethnicities, and economic backgrounds. That spirit of inclusiveness extended to my father's partnership with my mother. They were equals in every way. Although my father fulfilled the traditional role of bread-winner, it was Mom who handled the finances and managed the household. Dad's respect and admiration for my mother had an obvious influence on me. In their marriage and partnership they were role models in every way.

They raised five of us—four brothers and myself. On a modest income, they put all of us through college and ensured that we all graduated debt-free. Now that I think about it, college wasn't an option for any us. It was a re-quirement.

As important as formal education was in our family, family dinners were perhaps even more important in helping me learn and in shaping my values. We were expected to come to dinner well versed on the news of the day and prepared to discuss and defend our views on contentious issues. Eating was secondary. Dinner became an intellectual exercise in courage, communications, decisiveness, and especially values.

To say that values were important to my dad may be the understatement of all time. During our dinner debates, we could hold any view we wanted as long as it was consistent with a core set of beliefs that put a premium on integrity, honesty, social justice, and loyalty to God, family, and country. As long as we embraced these values and got an education, we were encouraged to become whatever we wanted, explore any road that beckoned us, chase any dream that produced passion in us, and strive to leave the world a little better than we found it.

That's what jarred me about the chance comment of that family friend. Would my father be proud that his daughter became CEO of a large company? Maybe. But there is no question he would be prouder still that I've tried to reflect his values, that I have a marriage he and my mom would recognize as consistent with their own, and that we've raised two great sons who will carry on his belief in the inherent goodness and potential of every human being.

Is it a shame my father didn't see my business success? Not one bit. The shame is that he's not here to witness the impact his values have had on me. That's what would make him proud and that's why it saddens me that he's gone.

■ ■ ■

Anne Mulcahy is chairman and chief
executive officer of Xerox Corporation.

Thomas Dolan, was an editor at pub-
lishing houses in New York.

Nancy Perot Mulford

■ Ross Perot

ONE OF MY most cherished memories of childhood is of riding in front of my father while he rode his beautiful Tennessee Walking Horse. An accomplished horseman, Dad folded his arms around me and around the pasture we went. As we rode, he made up clever, funny poems about me to the steady rhythm of the horse's hooves hitting the ground. I will never forget that feeling of security and being absolutely awash in love and affection. To this day, the security and love that my father gave to each of his five children has been the solid foundation from which we have learned to live and establish our own lives.

Anyone who really knows Ross Perot knows that he is first and foremost a family man. We knew with unquestioning certainty that we were the most important priority in his life. He expressed this dedication to us through his words—always taking time to compliment us and tell us how much he loved us—but, more importantly, through his actions. Somehow, through the demands of building a business and handling his considerable responsibilities, he was always available for us. We could always reach him if we needed to talk to him and very rarely did he miss being home for dinner. My parents made family dinner a high priority. Probably more than any other place, our sense of family, our identities, and our values were shaped as the seven of us gathered around our oval dining room table.

Ours was a magical childhood filled with a menagerie of pets and all kinds of trips and adventures. Dad has a wonderful imagination and a great sense of fun and he was always scheming up a fun, new project or plan. We spent countless hours playing in the elaborate multi-tiered treehouse that he and my brother built high up in the boughs of a huge oak tree. On the weekends, he took groups of our friends to the lake house and taught them all how to water ski. Dad made sure we all learned to snow ski and now three generations of our family ski together with Dad always in the lead, racing ahead of the pack down the mountain.

It is a tremendous privilege to have grown up with a man like Ross Perot for a father. He is truly extraordinary in both his public and private life, and I continue to learn from him and be inspired by his example each day. His high ideals and principles guide every decision he makes. His deep patriotism taught me a reverence for this country and a deep appreciation for all of those who are dedicated to protecting our freedom. His generosity and selfless service to others taught me how much difference one individual can make. His self-discipline inspires me to maintain the highest standards for myself. His deep yet quiet faith has been a powerful example to me of the importance of keeping religion and Christian principles at the center of my life.

Dad has led a life of remarkable achievement. Books have been written about him, movies have been made about him, and he has received countless awards and honors for his patriotism, business success, and philanthropy. But he often will say that his true measure of success will be if his children turn out to be good people and good citizens of this country.

I can assure you that we all love and admire him too much ever to disappoint him.

■ ■ ■

Nancy Perot Mulford was born in Dallas, Texas, and is the oldest of Ross and Margot Perot's four daughters. She is a graduate of Vanderbilt University, worked in the Reagan Administration, and is currently a writer and contributing editor to Veranda magazine. She is married to Clay Mulford and they have four sons.

Ross Perot was born in Texarkana, Texas, graduated from the United States Naval Academy, and later founded Electronic Data Systems, one of the premier information processing companies in the world. In 1988 he founded Perot Systems, of which he currently serves as Chairman Emeritus. He ran for president of the United States as an Independent candidate in 1992 and 1996. His honors include the Distinguished Graduate Award from the United States Naval Academy, the Winston Churchill Award, the Raoul Wallenberg Award, the Thomas Jefferson Award, the Eisenhower Award, and the Department of Defense Medal for Distinguished Public Service.

Lisa Murkowski

■ FRANK MURKOWSKI

GROWING UP in a noisy family of six kids, I learned early that you really have to speak up in life to be heard. But here's another lesson I learned: You really have to listen, too.

There was no such thing as a peaceful dinner hour in the Murkowski household. We always ate together, no matter what was on anyone's school or social agenda. As forks and plates clattered, so did eight voices.

From the head of the table, Dad ordered the topic of the evening.

Opinions from all were required, regardless of age or wisdom. Going around the table in age order, we would offer our thoughts on anything from the weekend's plans to what we'd be when we grew up to how oil development could be managed to the state's best advantage. I remember one night when Dad explained a troubling work situation, and one by one we gave our thoughts on whether he should fire the wayward employee. I often wondered what that employee would think if he knew his career was influenced by advisors who weren't old enough to drive!

There was never any question, though, that he would find out; one of the cardinal rules in the family was "Never repeat anything you hear at the dinner table." That policy gave my dad a sounding board for worries, dreams, and wild ideas, and it gave us kids the opportunity to speak freely without being criticized for intruding on grown-up affairs.

On the other hand, anyone was free to point out holes in an argument. The conversation ping-ponged back and forth across the plates, as we learned to listen, challenge and (sometimes) accept one another's ideas. At the end of the evening, there were no winners or losers. No one carried a grudge away from the dinner table. The shouting and disagreements weren't personal; they were just a way to sound out all sides of an idea.

Perhaps Dad placed so much value on his children's opinions because he had grown up as an only child and knew the value of being taken seriously by adults. Our nights around the dinner table instilled a deep self-confidence in each of us kids, and in the value of our own ideas. I don't think it ever crossed my mind that there might be something I couldn't do.

To this day, we gather as a family (now twenty-six including spouses and grandkids) several times a year, coming from all parts of the country. I count my brothers and sisters as my best friends. We still have long and noisy dinners, and, on the important things in life, we go around the table in age order, each expressing an opinion. We may not agree with one another, but every voice is heard. My father is the governor of Alaska and was a U.S. Senator for twenty-two years. He listens as attentively to his four-year-old grandson as he does to his daughter the U.S. Senator.

A parent who listens—really listens—to a child can shape the future. I always knew my dad believed in me.

∎ ∎ ∎

Lisa Murkowski is the first Alaskan woman to hold national office and the first Alaskan born Senator to serve the State. As the newly elected Governor of Alaska, her father, Governor Frank Murkowski, chose her to fill the Senate seat he vacated in 2002.

With years of experience in state and local politics, Lisa Murkowski quickly set to work on the economic and infrastructure projects important to her constituents, winning re-election to a full six-year term in the U.S. Senate in 2004. She and her husband Verne Martell, a small business owner, have two teenage sons, Nicolas and Matthew.

Frank Murkowski was elected Governor for the State of Alaska on November 5, 2002. A banker and former Alaska Commissioner of Economic Development, he first won election to the U.S. Senate in 1980 and was re-elected three times. During his twenty-two year tenure in the U.S. Senate, Murkowski served as chairman of the Energy Committee. Born in Seattle, Washington and raised in Ketchikan, Alaska, he and his wife Nancy have six children and fourteen grandchildren.

Peggy Noonan

■ JIM NOONAN

MY FATHER had a tough life. He was a working-class Brooklyn kid born in 1926, an only child whose father died when he was young. He and his mother went on what was then called relief. It was the middle of the Depression. He went to work early—odd jobs, paper routes, errand boy at local stores. He didn't finish high school. He didn't have any family but his mother, and she was not able to give him much. He had to do it all alone. He had to teach himself to be a man. He had to teach himself to be a person. One of the best times in his life was World War II, because he was surrounded by people who were on his side. Another great time was after the war, when he was a merchant seaman. Again there was a mission, again ca-maraderie. Afterward he married, had children, became a furniture salesman at department stores, struggled, divorced, worked, roamed. He never quite achieved the happiness he sensed was out there, and possible, and enjoyed by other people.

But when I think of my father my memories aren't sad. They're full of ex-pectation.

Here's the first thing I think of. My father is tying his tie. He's snapping the folds. He's humming, singing lyrics, and saying "Go baby, go" as he listens to the radio. It's Gene Krupa on a drum solo, or some big band thing—Tommy Dorsey, or "String of Pearls"—or a pop song of the fifties that's good. He has seen to it—he may have done the ironing—that his white shirt is per-fectly pressed. His shirttail is hanging outside his trousers, and his trousers are unbuttoned at the top because soon he will tuck the shirt in, but not right away. He doesn't want wrinkles. He doesn't want folds. He wants to go as long as possible without creases.

This is the fifties. I'm six or eight or nine. I'm watching him in the mir-ror. He is lost in his world of music.

He has showered. He shaves with a straight razor. He had fun lathering up. He had slapped on Mennen Old Spice aftershave, slapping it on, slap slap slap, so that it sounds like a turn-of-the-century barber stropping a razor on a piece of leather. He brushes his shoes with thick black paste and a wooden brush—strop strop again—and he shines them with a sock he took out of the hamper. He combs his black hair straight back. He looks in the mirror. He looks perfect, like Dana Andrews. He is a handsome man—six foot tall, slim, high cheekbones, deep brown eyes. He is a thirty-five-year-old furniture salesman at EJ Korvettes on Long Island. He has four kids (he will have seven) and a wife and a mortgage and lives in a flat in Long Island. It isn't compressed, like the city he came from. The suburbs are new then. The trees and lawns haven't filled out. It is gray and spare and not prosperous, as it is now. It is more modest, and sad. It is the fifties. Everyone has post-traumatic stress disorder (the Depression, the war, their rough immigrant parents) and doesn't know it. He doesn't really love his life—he's got the blues, grew up with too much loneliness and want, wanted to be an actor, to go to Hollywood, like Harry Guardino, who came from the old neighborhood in Brooklyn and made it big as a character actor. But it never worked out. He got married, babies came, he was moving couches and chairs. But: Listen to this music!

He was teaching me, though he did not know it: Life has compensations. Life can be fun. Music is a joy of life. Going out on Saturday night is a joy of life. Getting ready to go out is a joy. Having the shirt be crisp and the shoes be shined is a joy.

This is what I'm learning as I'm watching: Life has joys within it even if you don't find life to be generally joyous. It's good to go out and see the neighbors at the bar and pizza joint across town.

My father didn't know it but he was teaching me the joy of going out and having a good time.

This is the second thing I think of when I think of my father. It's the 1970s and he's standing at the stove making scrambled eggs. It's Sunday morning. We're in New Jersey. He is drinking Gallo wine, smoking, and making breakfast. He's got the stereo going full blast even though nobody's up but him and my youngest sisters, who are at the same moment blasting a cartoon show on TV. But my father doesn't hear it. He's turning bacon and listening to Judy Garland at Carnegie Hall. (He's saying, "Sing it, baby!" He's saying, to my six-year-old sister, "That's a Nelson Riddle arrangement.") He's singing with Judy. "Clang clang clang went the trolley" and "The night is bitter, the stars have lost their glitter. . . ." After that he puts on another LP, *West Side Story*, the movie version. He loves the dance at the gym, hits the fork against the pan, sings along to "America" and "Officer Krupke." He's remembering being a Shark, and a Jet. He's in his boxer shorts and an undershirt and bare feet on linoleum and he's in heaven. He's making food and listening to real artists. I come down from my room and have coffee and look at the papers.

He is teaching me: Art and entertainment are good and can elicit from within you real happiness, an enjoyment of the moment that . . . transcends.

This is the third thing I think of. It's the early sixties. I'm watching *Million Dollar Movie* on Channel 9. It's the start of the movie, the boring part where they put the names of everyone. I say something like, "I wish it would start." He instructs me. No, he says. "This is important. That's called the credits. You see who directed. If it's John Ford it's gonna be a good movie. You see who wrote it. You get to know who makes good movies. Watch those names."

He's teaching me: It's not all magic, things don't just happen, somebody worked on it, somebody did it, and the ones who do good work get a reputation for good work.

This is the fourth thing I think of. It's the 1950s and I am little. It is Friday night. My father is sitting on the couch watching the Friday night fights. There's a theme song: *To look sharp da da DA da da—To FEEL sharp—da da DA da da*. He is leaning forward on the couch. His knee is bopping up and down with tension and excitement. The fights are about to begin. It's the great heyday of the ethnic guys of the cities of the East—Jake LaMotta, Rocky Graziano, Rocky Marciano. They are tough, ready young guys with names like our neighbors. Sugar Ray Robinson. My father has four kids, all girls, and he has no one to watch the fights with, but I want to sit next to my father on the couch and I want to root with him so I decide I like the fights. He tells me about what it was like on the radio when he was a kid, what it was like when Joe Louis beat Max Schmeling, what it was like when that son of a bitch Max Baer went down.

The fight begins. My father always has a favorite. "He's gonna kill that guy by the third round. This is gonna be a TKO, this guy can last forever, watch." My father is moving his shoulders, feinting, making a fist. Sometimes he stands and shouts, "Go baby, go!"

He doesn't know it but he is teaching me that there's an outward world where things happen, where you can become engaged and get excited and take a side and root for your guy. He is teaching me a fight isn't bad, it's human; it's how we are.

He is teaching me, again, about the compensating pleasures of being alive.

He died in 1999. If he could see me writing this he'd say, "That's what you remember?"

I'd say, "Yeah."

He'd ponder this and say, "Good."

Then he'd say, "Ya got some music here?" (I do.) He'd say, "What're ya doing for fun?" (I'd say "Going out to see friends.") He'd say, "Anything on TV?" (I'd say, "Something. Let's channel surf—that's what they call it now—we'll find something.")

■ ■ ■

Peggy Noonan is a contributing editor to the Wall Street Journal, *and a columnist for the Journal's online editorial page. She is the author of seven books, including* John Paul the Great, When Character Was King, *and* The Case Against Hillary Clinton.

Jim Noonan (below, second from right) was, consecutively, a merchant seaman, a counterman in a bakery, an appliance salesman in department stores, and a furniture salesman. He liked merchant seaman best. He died six years ago.

Courtesy of Kate Burton

Sandra Day O'Connor

■ HARRY DAY

GIRLS OFTEN are particularly close to their fathers. It was true for me. I grew up on a remote cattle ranch in the high desert region on the Arizona/New Mexico border. I was the first child of my parents and their only child for nine years.

My early years brought me in close contact with my parents all day, every day. As a rancher my father worked out of his house. We sat at the table together for three meals a day unless the ranch work kept my father out on a distant part of the ranch all day long. There were things to be done constantly on different parts of the rather large ranch. It might be a damaged fence or gate. It could be a cow with an infected eye, or a little calf without a mother, or a cow stuck in the mud in a bog.

My father liked to have company when he had hours to drive in the truck or jeep to reach the location where some repair or work was needed. I was usually that "company." Sometimes I preferred to stay home and read, but DA, as I called him, said ,"You'd better go with me, Sandra. I saw something unusual that you will want to see."

"Oh, what is it, DA? Tell me!"

"No, you'll just have to go along and see it for yourself."

Faced with that choice, I agreed to go with my father, sometimes for a very long day. But he, as promised, showed me some unusual or special thing, such as a bird nest with some little eggs in it, or a newly found sample of ancient Indian petroglyphs, or a herd of antelope. He liked to talk and there was a stream of conversation throughout the day ranging from practical to the academic. The relationship we had was very strong. Spending hours discussing ranching, politics, and economics was a treat that many young people do not experience.

DA expected not only the cowboys but also his children and any visiting cousins to do a share of the ranch work and to do it well. He wanted any task, however small, to be accomplished in a competent and professional manner. If we did not do the job well enough, he did not scold us, but it was clear when he thought it was not well done. As a result, we worked hard and did our best to receive a brief nod of approval from DA.

I remember one occasion when I was about fourteen. The spring round-up was going on, which required about a month of pre-dawn to dusk days when the round-up crew rode horseback over a different area each day to gather the cattle and brand the calves. The round-up cook could not be there one day and I offered to drive the truck with the lunch to the place the crew would be in the late morning, branding cattle. It was a rather remote place with a very bad trail for a road. I loaded the truck with all the food, utensils, coffee pot, and everything needed and started the trip early in the morning. Partway to my destination the truck had a flat tire. There was no going on or going back until the tire was changed. No one would be coming along who could help. I was miles from any other person.

I got the jack out of the truck and with every bit of strength I could muster managed to jack up the truck to get the tire off the ground. But I could not loosen the lug bolts. They had probably never been removed and years of dust and rust held them immovable. Finally, in desperation I stood on the arm of the lug wrench to add all my body weight to the task. It worked. The lug bolt turned slightly. At last I was able to get it off. Then I had to do the same thing with all the other bolts. It took a couple hours for me to get the tire changed.

As a result of the flat tire I arrived at the round-up destination about two hours later than expected but I was rather proud of myself for having been able to change the tire. The cowboys and my father were already there with a large herd of cattle. I put the lunch out, built a fire, and made some coffee.

DA saw me when I arrived but he continued working with the cattle and did not stop for lunch. He did not stop the work until all the branding was complete. By then all the men were very tired, hungry, and thirsty. They quickly ate everything I had brought.

"You're late," said DA.

"I know," I said. "I had a flat tire and had to change it."

"You should have started earlier," said DA.

"Sorry, DA. I didn't expect a flat."

I had expected a word of praise for changing the tire. But, to the contrary, I realized that only one thing was expected: an on-time lunch. No excuses accepted.

Looking back I think the lessons I learned of personal responsibility and no excuses accepted were good ones and served me well later in life. My father's work ethic and values were good ones, and my love and respect for him never wavered. He was a great role model.

■ ■ ■

Sandra Day O'Connor's career as the 102nd Supreme Court Justice began with her appointment by President Ronald Reagan on September 25, 1981. She is the author of Lazy B, The Majesty of the Law, *and* Chico.

Harry Day grew up on the Lazy B Ranch in southern Arizona and New Mexico

■ TIP O'NEILL

IT DID NOT MATTER that we lived in one of the most densely populated congressional districts in the country; Dad firmly believed that kids and animals belonged together. My mother was not quite so sure. To her horror, the day the first of their five children were born, Dad went out and bought a black Labrador retriever puppy. He could not imagine his newborn daughter growing up without a dog. Dubhin (Irish for Little Black) soon outgrew my parents' small, rented apartment in North Cambridge, Massachusetts, and was sent packing to my grandparents' house in the exurbs. But that was only the beginning of our experiences with animals in the heart of a working-class city neighborhood. We went through a series of dogs, rabbits, chickens, fish, and turtles.

During one Easter in the '50s, Dad decided that he would surprise us with some Easter eggs. When the five of us awoke to look for the baskets, we were directed to a large cardboard box in the kitchen. In it were a dozen chicken eggs. Dad wanted us to "experience" the excitement of new life as these chickens were hatched. The eggs had to be kept warm, of course, so Dad concocted an incubator in the overheated but well-lit laundry room. By this time our family of seven had grown into a thirteen-room house. Day and night, we went down the steps to the cellar to watch the chickens hatch. It was thrilling to see them peck their way into the world. In his daily call from Washington to check in with Mama and the family, we reported seeing first one, then another, then six, then eight, getting bigger and bigger. Who knew that chickens could grow so fast? Soon, they, too, were banished from the house.

But mostly we had dogs: first, Dubhin; then a Dalmation, Spot; next, Duke, a real live "pedigree" mongrel. One day when Dad called, Mama reported that a hit and run driver had killed Duke in front of our home. We had to watch as my brother Tom moved the bloodied body of our beloved Duke. Dad, in Washington, was of course concerned about how his young brood was surviving this ordeal. Mama did not want another dog and warned us not to go on about Duke's death when Dad came home. After all, she knew she would be the one to care for another dog. And coping with five children when Dad was away in Washington during the work week was quite enough for her. Of course, our brave fronts crumbled the moment we saw him. Amid manipulative tears, we reported in graphic detail the terrible crime and our great loss. We watched Dad hopefully as he scoured the *Boston Globe* for "Dogs for Sale."

If Dad was away from us during the week in Washington, he was all ours on the weekend. He reserved Saturday mornings for errands. Constituents "accidentally" caught up with him when he was on his so-called "ethnic walk." He took notes on their requests as he proceeded from the supermarket, owned by an Armenian American, to the Chinese laundry, to the Italian barber and cobbler, and to the Irish-American butcher. Then, in the afternoon, off the family went to see a football game at Boston College. Or he took each of us in turn to the Fresh Pond public course to instruct us in the royal game of golf. Sundays, after Mass, depending on the season, he brought us sledding or ice skating, or we went swimming at the beach, or just for a ride for an ice cream cone.

The Sunday after Duke died, Dad packed the kids in the car to go for a ride. Mama may have been tipped off by the newspaper she saw bulging out of his jacket pocket. Her last words, before we took off, were, "Remember, no dog." We badgered him to tell us where we were going, but he refused to say. Crowded into the car, we left Cambridge and headed north, through the congested suburbs of Medford, Malden, and Woburn, into the country, past the Topfield fairgrounds. After two hours, we finally stopped at Ipswich-by-the-sea. The sign on the road leading to the farm said "Beagles for Sale."

Fenced in a bin on the front lawn of the farmhouse was a mother beagle with about half a dozen pups. The farmer told us that most of the week-old pups had already been promised to others, and that only one or two were still available. The smallest, the runt of the litter, looked up at us, his eyes expectant. He, of course, had not yet been chosen. In response to Dad's questions, the owner said that, yes, the puppies were young, but they had all their shots, and could be taken away from the mother. We opted for the youngest, frailest, sweetest looking. Pokey.

Dad gently wrapped Pokey in an old towel and, moving the ever-present loose cigars and newspapers, placed him in the front seat of the car. Next came the question of who would sit in the coveted front seat next to Dad and the dog. It was easily resolved. Dad stopped the car every fifteen minutes so we could change seats and each could have his time with Pokey. It was dark by the time we got home. Mama was almost ready with the Sunday roast dinner.

I can't say she was surprised. She was partly angry and partly resigned. We swore that we would feed, water, and walk the dog; on our honor, Mama would not have to do a thing. Together, she and Dad made a shelter for Pokey. He was shaking, and we wanted to keep him as warm as possible. The vet later told us that the farmer should never have sold a pup that young away from his mother. We covered Pokey in blankets and made sure that a ticking clock, resembling a mother's heartbeat, was placed close to him. Feeding was no problem. We certainly did have baby bottles in the house. Each of us was given a turn at gently holding the pup to feed it. Mama was Pokey's safety net. Daily she reminded us of our pledge, and we dutifully fed him Hill's horsemeat for dogs, and walked him on the leash. Dad, away during the week, was exempt from the daily chores.

Soon Pokey was playing with the kids outside; as he became familiar with the neighborhood, we eventually let him go without a leash. There was only one problem with this free-living policy. When the moon was high and full, Pokey came home late, went to the intersection on the corner where we lived, and howled. This routinely happened on a monthly basis at one o'clock in the morning. Horrified at the prospect that Pokey disturbed the neighbors, my father jumped out of bed to go after him. This was Pokey's great game. Dad, in pajamas and overcoat, got into the car, drove the quarter of a block to the intersection, and opened the car door. Pokey could not resist the possibility of exploring further afield in a car, and in he hopped. Dad collared him and brought him into the house.

Dad and Pokey had a lot in common. As they both grew, their worlds expanded. Both had a wonderful curiosity and a love of people. Pokey followed us to school, visited neighbors, stayed overnight with our baby sitter, Anne O'Connor, fifteen blocks away. Sometimes he stayed away for weeks at a time, wandering who knows where, but always to return. Dad traveled throughout the world. He went from being a master of constituent services, legislative protocol, and New England regional issues to deal with the great national questions of the economy, civil rights, Vietnam, and energy, to name but a few.

He met thousands of people around this country and in other lands. No matter how far he went, however, Dad treasured his base: his family, the people of North Cambridge and those of the Eighth Congressional District of Massachusetts. Both Dad and Pokey loved us deeply, but they did not "belong" to us. They belonged to a wider world.

■ ■ ■

Susan O'Neill is the president of Susan O'Neill & Associates a Washington, DC, firm specializing in non-profit fundraising and special events production. Her professional career has included teaching in public schools, heading a Training and Education Division for a national labor union and organizing national political campaigns. She is the mother of one daughter, Michaela Daniel.

Thomas P. (Tip) O'Neill, Jr. was a Member of Congress from the 8th Congressional District of Massachusetts. He served in Congress from 1953 until 1987. During his Congressional career, Mr. O'Neill served as Majority Whip, Majority Leader, and served the longest consecutive term as Speaker of the House of Representatives from 1977 until 1987

Maureen Orth

■ KARL ORTH

WHEN BOYS first started taking notice of me or I of them, my father scared them to death. He was a big, tall, handsome, former college football star tackle and his handshake literally crushed theirs. They would come to the door to pick me up, meet my dad, who always imposed a strict curfew, and then walk out of the house shaking their hands out at their sides. I was never taken home late!

Karl Orth never treated me in any way special because I was a girl. I was the eldest and supposed to set an example. If I complained that someone in the neighborhood had picked a fight or hit me, my father's advice was, "Hit 'em back." He expected good grades but never got involved in homework. Nevertheless, he would drill me over and over for my Baltimore Catechism lessons in the precepts of Catholicism. Because I went to public schools in California, every Saturday from the age of four to thirteen I had to attend catechism class presided over by an ancient nun who kept order with a wooden clicker and, when that didn't work, by twisting ears. My father was a very devout Catholic and the lessons had to be perfect. From an early age he stressed that there was always plenty of time for dating and marriage; the most important thing was to get an education.

I attended Berkeley in the sixties—we lived nearby—and you could probably write a historical outline of the issues and headlines then just by the arguments that my dad and I had over politics. I once brought my mother to hear Mario Savio, the leader of the Free Speech Movement, when he was running for the Senate in 1970, and the Black Panthers passed around a collection plate. My father came to pick her up, and, when he heard from the cop outside what was going on inside, he refused to speak to me for three days. Yet my dad was very popular with my friends. They loved to come over and hear our fights at the dinner table and marveled at the free-wheeling debate we always seemed to have. It took a great deal of restraint for my dad to allow me to join the Peace Corps right after college and to be sent to live in a poor barrio in Medellín, Colombia, a place none of us had ever heard of. Yet when he came to the dedication of a school I helped build there—named for me—I think I knew he was proud of me. I say "I think" because he never said the words. Typically, he told me I should consider accepting the proposal of my rich Colombian boyfriend. That way, "You could really help the people here." I wasn't sure my own happiness was part of the equation. Marriage had never been discussed before, but, now that college was done and the Peace Corps nearly over, what was my logical next step?

Poor Daddy. I confounded him. A few years later when we were driving together, he pulled his station wagon over to the curb and out of the blue asked me if I was planning to marry my old college sweetheart who was still hanging around. I said no. Then he asked about the dashing Colombian. I said no again. He turned to me and said, "Then maybe you have a late vocation." No, Daddy, no.

Sadly, my father died suddenly of a heart attack a few days shy of his fifty-eighth birthday. He never lived to see that I finally did marry a strong German/Irish Catholic quick with words, not so different than he was.

■ ■ ■

Maureen Orth is a special correspondent for Vanity Fair *and the author of* The Importance of Being Famous. *She is married to Tim Russert, moderator of* Meet the Press, *and is the mother of Luke Russert, co-host of* 60-20 *on XM Radio.*

Karl Orth, a beer distributor, died in 1973 while giving a speech opposing rent control in Berkeley.

Nancy Reagan

■ LOYAL DAVIS

FROM THE EARLIEST years I can remember, my father, Dr. Loyal Davis, was an inspiring presence in my life. As a prominent physician in Chicago, he was well respected by the community and always carried himself with the utmost dignity and respect. He never lost sight that his patients were real people—often facing very difficult challenges.

When I visited his office, or listened to him recall his day around the family dinner table, I was always touched by the compassion he had for others and his extensive knowledge about a wide variety of subjects. He loved to discuss serious issues, and our household discussions were always stimulating and challenging. Analytical, warm, and wise, I can clearly remember my father's definition of happiness. "Nancy," he said, "the answer to that question is almost twenty-five centuries old, and it's basically what the Greeks said. Happiness is the pursuit of excellence in all aspects of one's life."

My father felt passionately about his work. He taught me to value one's dedication to one's profession, to respect diligence and integrity, and to embrace the importance of knowledge. But despite the obligations he faced in his medical practice, he always had time for me. And he had that unique fatherly gift of being able to make his daughter feel that she was the "center of his universe."

As I grew older and began pursuing my own career, one of the things I valued most about my father was that he frequently and consistently wrote letters. While I was away at college, acting in Hollywood, First Lady of California, and First Lady of the United States, I could always count on a wonderful letter from him. Whether to convey a message or just to keep in touch, I cherished each letter he sent.

Recently, I found a letter from my father from almost sixty-five years ago. I was attending Smith College when I received this letter just before

Christmas. In it my father said the most touching things about his love for me, and the support he would always give. He wrote, "I want you to know that I'm always ready to help in any way I can." And he meant it. For the rest of his life, he always offered his help and advice.

I am so happy I found this letter. It reminded me of so many that he sent. I encourage everyone to save the letters sent by their parents—one day they will truly be treasured.

■ ■ ■

Former First Lady *Nancy Reagan* currently lives in Los Angeles, California.

Dr. *Loyal Davis* was one of the most respected physicians in the United States. A neurosurgeon, he held the Chair of the Department of Surgery at Northwestern University Medical School for over thirty years, and served as Editor in Chief of the Journal of the American College of Surgeons. He authored many books, including several novels, as well as numerous articles on surgery.

Julia Reed

■ CLARKE REED

MY FAVORITE PICTURE of my father was taken on October 10, 1973, the day Spiro Agnew resigned as Richard Nixon's vice president. He'd been somewhere in his small plane, a Piper Aztec six-seater, and a photographer from our local Greenville, Mississippi, paper snapped him as he stepped out onto the wing. He had on pin-striped suit pants with his usual red-and-black suspenders and monogrammed button-down shirt; under one arm was his jacket, a flight map, and a copy of the *Wall Street Journal*. But the most striking thing about the photograph is the fact that he has an enormous grin on his face.

It wasn't that he found Agnew's forced resignation remotely entertaining—after all, he'd had a considerable hand in getting Nixon elected, twice. Also, Agnew was a conservative, and the closest thing to a Southerner a national Republican ticket was going to get in those days, both facts guaranteed to make Clarke Reed's true-believing heart beat a little faster. But there were two other things at work. First—unlike the departed veep—most of the time he enjoyed the press, who were waiting for him on the tarmac. Second, and by far the more important, he knew he was about to put on his "act."

My father's act, a mixture of great charm, understated erudition, and self-effacing humor, is a mighty impressive thing. I have seen him put it on to disarm adversaries, placate allies, create illusions, or just to entertain himself. In this particular instance he expressed outrage that the Democratic Speaker of the House had not allowed the vice president a public hearing. (Outrage, along with indignation and castigation, can be a useful part of the act, especially when dealing with recalcitrant administrations or anybody remotely hesitant about contributing money to some noble cause or another.) Then he tossed out a bit of intimate info gleaned from a dinner conversation with Agnew, and wound up typically upbeat, noting that the already beleaguered president (whom he always called "the prez" in private) would now be able to get on with the business of running the country.

His friend Hodding Carter III once wrote that Daddy had managed to build the Southern Republican party with "mirrors and smoke," making it seem more important than it really was for just long enough that the reality came to match the perception. The solid, segregated South had been isolated politically and economically for a century, and the act was critical in the process of building not just a Republican party, but a modern two-party system that might finally end our long stretch as a national joke. He and Hodding, the editor of our paper and a liberal Democrat, often joined forces, staging dramatic mock debates for the benefit of the suddenly curious national press. Hodding argued in favor of the Loyalist Democratic Party (i.e., not the party of Ross Barnett and Jim Eastland) and Daddy argued in favor of the Republicans (all of whom, it was said, correctly in those days, could fit into a phone booth), and they passed a bottle of Scotch between them while standing, usually, on top of a table in our living room. It was such a good act that Bill Buckley put them on Firing Line, albeit without the Scotch or the table.

Irony is no small part of the act. In the midst of the Vietnam War, he told me good night by opening my bedroom door a crack, grinning, and uttering the single word "peace," though he was hardly on the side of the antiwar protesters. He still says "peace," along with "press on" (sometimes "press on to greater things"), "abbreducci," (the version of arrivederci that Louis Armstrong employs in "High Society") and "keep it in the road." One of his favorite parting lines is, "It's been a little piece of paradise," the point being, of course, that sometimes it has definitely not been. Either way, he is prone to accompanying his departure with a twirl of his finger in the air, or a click of his heels or both. There is a deep current of generosity running through the act—few are left un-entertained because there are few events he doesn't think could benefit from an injection of pizzazz (another of this favorite words), which he is always happy to provide.

He traveled all the time when I was young, and when I'd ask him where he'd been he'd always say "saving the free world." It was another line that he'd utter with that Johnny Carson-esque straight face barely holding back a grin, but he also believed it. He believed in Right over Left and the West over Communism. (I was the only child in elementary school, or possibly the world, who had been read aloud the entire works of Whittaker Chambers be-

fore turning nine.) But he's also a realist—the Justice Department ran the field operations that integrated Mississippi's public schools from the apartment above his office; now he's an environmentalist who founded Mississippi Wildlife—and his political instincts are always on the money. After hurricane Camille ravaged the Mississippi Gulf Coast in 1969, Nixon planned a fly-over of the destruction. Daddy told White House Aide Bryce Harlow that if the president didn't stop and get out of the plane, then he shouldn't bother to come at all—a lesson another president would have done well to learn a few decades later. Nixon did stop, becoming the first sitting president to set foot on Mississippi soil since Roosevelt's hunting trip, and later the state gave him his biggest margin of reelection.

He took me to see Nixon that day. He took me, thank God, pretty much, everywhere—but, before I was old enough to go, he always brought me stuff, usually procured at the last minute from the Memphis airport gift shop. One such gift was a stuffed buzzard, made of black fur with purple felt wings and a lavender head with rheumy yellow plastic eyes. "Buzzard" also had a long elastic band attached to his head so he could hang menacingly from the ceiling, but I preferred to sleep with him, which I did so often that my mother was constantly patching his worn-out head. I loved Buzzard because he was, well, cool, and no one in the world could have given him to me but my father. Had he come home that day with, say, a curly-haired baby doll, I would have been completely dumbfounded, even at six.

My father's accomplishments have had lasting repercussions and his principled stands have sometimes cost him. But, even in trying times, he has almost always managed to enjoy himself—a lot—and, more importantly, to laugh at himself. He freely admits that he is usually his own best audience. There have been countless times when he has nudged me on the shoulder and whispered that he was about to dive into some group somewhere because it was time to "put my act on 'em." Finally I came to realize that he, the force of his personality, is the act.

At his surprise sixtieth birthday party we celebrated him and the real, show-biz acts that he put on as an Air Force lieutenant running the Mobile, Alabama, officer's club, by recreating the best and worst of what he staged there. (Among the worst was a woman who tap-danced and clacked her false teeth in time to "Stars and Stripes Forever," an act harder than you'd think to recreate.) My friends and I were the Satin Dolls and it took two of us less than ten minutes to rewrite the entire lyrics to the song "Satin Doll," such was the richness of our material. The first line was "Silver haired cool cat, he slays me." Twenty years later, he still does. The act—the man—remains strong stuff.

■ ■ ■

Julia Reed is a contributing editor at Vogue *and* Newsweek *and the author of* Queen of the Turtle Derby and Other Southern Phenomena.

Clarke Reed, a businessman in Greenville, Mississippi, is the former chairman of the Mississippi Republican Party and founder of Mississippi Wildlife.

Diane Rehm

■ WADIE AED

MY FATHER died when I was nineteen, eleven months after my mother died. He was sixty-two. She was forty-nine. His heart was broken. She was the love of his life. He had come to this country from Lebanon in 1913, and had gone back to Egypt to beg her to marry him in 1929, even though she'd been engaged to someone else at the time. However, she consented, and left her entire family behind, to marry my father and come to the United States.

On Sundays when I was a young child, my father and I took the 16th Street bus together from our home in the Petworth section of Washington, downtown to 17th and P Street, to the homes of my three aunts, my father's sisters, all of whom lived within two blocks of one another. My dad used those moments on the bus to ask me about school and friends, always inquiring in a kind and interested way, wanting to connect with me and my life. That effort to connect was not easy, since our family life seemed so different from that of my friends.

My parents spoke primarily Arabic in the home. As I child, I understood most of what they said. But, as my father and I rode the bus together, I became resentful if he spoke to me in Arabic rather than English. I didn't want people around us hearing a strange language, and to know that we were somehow "different." So I responded to his questions in English, to establish my own identity, separating myself from him. I realize now that I was ashamed of our differences, ashamed that we were not like others, and wished desperately that we were.

The same was true of the food we ate. I remember that our house was filled with the wonderful aromas of Arabic foods that my mother prepared. My friends commented on the fragrances, and asked what kinds of foods were being served for dinner. But rather than feeling pride, I felt uncomfortable, knowing that the foods we ate were different from the ones in their homes, thereby establishing one more difference between my friends and me.

As soon as we arrived at the home of the first aunt, any embarrassment was forgotten. My cousins, all of whom were somewhat older than I, were delighted to see me, as were my aunts. And the most remarkable aspect of the visits was this: all three of the aunts were cooking the same main meal, be it chicken, lamb, beef, or fish. It took me a long time to realize that, since they all spoke with each other daily, they all knew exactly what the best buys of the week were, and they all made identical choices!

My father and his sisters sat around in the living room, shared the gossip of the Arab community, smoked cigarettes, nibbled on delicacies, and cautioned all of us children to try to keep down the gleeful noise and laughter. This was the time of the visit I loved most of all—a moment and place where I truly felt I belonged. All around me were my wonderful cousins, aunts, and uncles, whom I adored, we could make more noise than was allowed in my home, and my father was relaxed and enjoying the company of his sisters and their husbands.

Of course, they all wanted us to stay and have lunch with them. But that was not to be the case. My mother was waiting for us at home, having prepared her own special Sunday feast for us, and we never wanted to miss that. However loyal my father was to his older sisters, his greater loyalty was to my mother.

So, having spent an hour or so visiting with the aunts and cousins, back we rode, up 16th Street, to our own home and to Sunday lunch with our own family.

It's taken me many years to understand the importance of those moments with my father, my aunts, and my cousins, and to treasure the memories. I think those memories have helped me to appreciate not only the richness of my own background but to take pleasure in exploring the origins and differences in others, and to applaud them. I think my dad would enjoy knowing how important those visits were to me.

■ ■ ■

For 26 years, *Diane Rehm* has been host and executive producer of The Diane Rehm Show, *distributed nationally and internationally by NPR.*

Wadie Aed came to the United States from Beirut, Lebanon, in 1914. For many years he and his brothers owned a grocery store in Washington, DC He died in 1956, at age sixty-two.

Condoleezza Rice

■ JOHN W. RICE, JR.

I HAVE BECOME convinced over the years that there is no more important relationship for a girl than the one she has with her father. It is a girl's father who helps to shape her character, forms her trust, and I believe entirely sets her expectations of the way men should treat her. He defended me. He encouraged me. And he challenged me.

My father did everything in his power to protect me from harm or ridicule. When I was about seven or eight years old, my father wanted me to perform in my elementary school talent show. He hired the drama teacher to give me tap dancing lessons and bought me a costume. Needless to say, I was embarrassed because I was not very good. But on the day of the show, there was my father—with all of his imposing height, and weight, and strength—standing at my side and staring at the audience, as if daring them to laugh. No one made a sound, and then everyone applauded.

My father also encouraged me to explore all of my unique interests, ideas, and dreams. When I was eight years old, I decided that I wanted to join the Presbyterian Church. Never mind that this was a ceremony for adults, not children. I was drawn to the Church, and I wanted to join. My father, a Presbyterian minister, never discouraged me, or forbade me, or told me it was a stupid idea. To the contrary: He fully supported me. So, one Sunday morning, with my father looking on proudly, I walked down the aisle and joined the Presbyterian Church, which remains my spiritual home to this day.

What I am perhaps most grateful for is that my father continuously challenged me to improve myself—to study more, to work harder, to practice longer. He never let me think that certain goals were unattainable, or that my horizons were somehow limited. Once, while figure skating, I took a pretty bad fall. My father, however, just replied, "You'll be all right," and encouraged me to keep practicing. He loved me so much that he wanted me to have standards of excellence that inspired my dedication and sacrifice. That, he taught me, was the only way to fulfill your greatest aspirations.

More than anything, however, my father was always my friend. We watched football together, went to church together, and generally hung out together. He was my confidant and my counselor, the person I turned to first when I wanted to share some good news or needed to work through some bad times. We were always buddies. The memory of our relationship sustains me today. And there is nothing more that a girl could ever want from her father.

■ ■ ■

Condoleezza Rice is a classical pianist, a professor of political science, and a former Provost of Stanford University. She served as National Security Advisor to President George W. Bush until becoming Secretary of State in January 2005.

Reverend John W. Rice, Jr. was an educator, a religious leader, and, like his daughter, a sports enthusiast.

Rachel Ripken

■ CAL RIPKEN, JR.

FOR TWENTY-ONE YEARS my dad played major league baseball, a game that he knew well and one that was his life's passion.
Through hard work and dedication, he excelled at baseball—breaking
records, winning awards, and leaving a lasting impression on fellow players
and fans alike. People often say to me, "Wow, it must be so cool to have a
baseball player for a dad." When I think of my dad, however, I don't think of
the baseball aspect, but instead I think of him as a person, as my dad with
whom I've shared so many wonderful memories.

Family is really important to my dad. Despite a hectic baseball schedule
that naturally lent itself to much travel on the road, my dad found ways to include us and to let us know that he was thinking about us even during the
biggest moments of his career. I remember when I was five years old; my dad
was playing in his 2,131st consecutive game, one that would break the record
held by Lou Gehrig. My brother, Ryan, and I had made a T-shirt that read
"2,131 Hugs and Kisses for Daddy" and had given it to my dad that morning.
During the game my dad spontaneously ran over to us in the stands and took
off his jersey to reveal the T-shirt that we had made for him underneath his
uniform. He left his jersey and his hat with us, after planting huge kisses on
my mom, brother, and me. The fact that he was sweaty from the game (combined with the fact that I was only five) made me wipe off his kiss! I am still
reminded of that moment, not only because I have a picture of me wiping off
the kiss, but also because it was one of countless examples of how much my
dad values his family.

I also remember that day because it was my first day of real school, lower
school. My dad is big on "firsts." That day was a big "first" for him professionally, but he also saw that it was an important "first" for me. My dad took me to

school that morning and went on to make history later that day, but both "firsts" were very significant and meaningful to him.

Many people think of my dad as quiet, but he has an incredible sense of humor. Most baseball players have nicknames on their teams. We found out later in my dad's career that the trainers on the Orioles knew him as "The Annoying Man." I know "The Annoying Man" well, as his main joy in life is to embarrass and annoy me. I remember being in eighth grade in the school dance company at St. Paul's in Baltimore. My dad came to pick me up from practice and purposefully turned the music up as loud as possible so that when I opened the door everyone heard the music blaring. I could hear the music as I walked up to the car and stood there not opening the door for several minutes while he tried to get me to fall for his trick by opening the door. I was mortified. More recently, he picked me up after a basketball game. This time he poked his head out the sunroof and waved his arms around to get my attention. Everyone around me was laughing but more in appreciation of how great it was to have a dad with such a great sense of humor. I love him for that and he has even dubbed me "TAG"—"The Annoying Girl."

As a sophomore in high school, I am presenting my parents with a lot of new "firsts." I got my learner's permit to drive this summer, and my dad was the first person to ride in the car with me. His competitive nature comes out when we drive together, as we critique each other on our driving skills and he of course claims that he is the best driver on the road! Through each of these new experiences, my dad is a constant source of wisdom. He values my opinion and trusts my judgment in each decision that I make. Even though, unlike my brother, I have had no aspirations of being a professional baseball player, my father supports me in whatever I pursue. His advice has always been to do the things that make me happy. He has taught me that if you believe in a dream, you can accomplish it, and even more through a lot of hard work and perseverance.

In 2001, my whole family flew out to Seattle to watch my dad receive his second Most Valuable Player award during his last career All-Star game. Several Japanese reporters were at the game because Ichiro Suzuki, a Japanese baseball player, was a member of the All-Star team. My dad was introducing us to the reporters and, because I had taken Japanese for several years, I blurted out, "Konnichiwa," which means hello in Japanese. The reporters were so excited that I spoke their language that they asked if I wanted to say something about my dad. I of course panicked for a second, and then said in Japanese, "My name is Rachel Ripken and I'm happy for my dad." I was and continue to be so happy for all of his accomplishments—setting world records, having an amazing baseball career, but most importantly for the accomplishment of being a great dad and inspiring role model.

■ ■ ■

Rachel Ripken, daughter of baseball's "Ironman" Cal Ripken, Jr. lives in Hunt Valley, Maryland, where she is currently completing her sophomore year in high school. She enjoys the arts and acting and has appeared in several national television commercials and had a small part in a recent major motion picture. In addition, Rachel volunteers her time to help the Cal Ripken, Sr. Foundation for disadvantaged youth.

Cal Ripken, Jr. is owner and CEO of Ripken Baseball. His company owns and operates a pair of minor league teams, the Aberdeen Ironbirds and the Augusta Green Jackets. He also helps grow the game he loves at the grassroots level through youth baseball and softball academies in Aberdeen, Maryland, and Myrtle Beach, South Carolina. Ripken, a best-selling author who will release his third book in the spring of 2006, has a youth league of over 700,000 kids that bears his name worldwide.

Lynda Johnson Robb

■ LYNDON BAINES JOHNSON

MY FATHER called me his "3D girl," which stood for Daddy's Darling Daughter. I was born, very welcomed after nine years of marriage, while he was a congressman from Texas. Since Congress was in session, I was born in Washington, DC, instead of my parents' home state of Texas, and I've never been able to live it down!

Congress, both the House and the Senate, dominated my father's life, and mine, while I was growing up. The first half of my school year started in Texas when Congress was out of session, and each year ended in Washington, DC, where I transferred in January when the congressional session began. It seemed to me then that I had the worst of both worlds, for Texas schools started early in August, and DC schools finished late in June! Breaks, vacations, and weekends were spent in Daddy's office opening mail or giving tours to "constituents." I even sold Girl Scout cookies door to door in the Senate offices. The Capitol Building was my playground, much like today's kids hang out at the mall, and I knew more senators and their families then than I know now!

At home, when friends came to dinner, I sat on the living room floor and listened, bringing popcorn to "Uncle Sam" (Rayburn, long-time Speaker of the House) and others, like Senator Stu Symmington, "Uncle Dick" Russell, and Tommy "The Cork" Corcoran, whom I considered friends rather than important political figures. When there was to be an interesting debate on the Senate floor, my father would call school and have me excused so I could witness history rather than read about it. I was present when Alaska and Hawaii were admitted to the Union and I shared a step, sitting with Mrs. John Kennedy in an overfull gallery, for one congressional speech.

I even got to watch President Eisenhower's inauguration from Daddy's office window where I had a bird's eye view of the inaugural platform, which

faced the Supreme Court building. From my perch in a window seat, warm inside where I could drink a Coke, I opened the window to hear better and watched the long ceremony unfold in comfort. Since then I have been seated on the wintry, January inaugural platform to witness my own father, and Presidents Kennedy, Nixon, and Carter sworn in, but I have never spent a more comfortable inaugural than the one in 1953!

Although Daddy early on gave me the bug for politics by including me in his world, he missed out on a lot of my world growing up, and, as he aged, he regretted missing milestones like field days. So it is for many fathers who only realize what they've missed when they become grandfathers. Always one to love a grand surprise, one of Daddy's last Christmases he dressed up like Santa Claus and rode up to the ranch on a bright green lawn mower, pulling a wagonload of toys. My daughters and some of the ranch children huddled close at all the loud noise until his five-year-old granddaughter, Lucinda, announced, "That's not Santa. That's my Boppa!" and the children drew close.

One of my most treasured photos of my father is not one of him with me, but one of him with my two oldest girls snuggling in his arms, as he sits in his most comfortable recliner reading "The Night Before Christmas" to them, something he never had time to do with me!

■ ■ ■

Lynda Johnson Robb is a professional volunteer who has served on numerous boards and governmental commissions, most recently as chairman of Reading Is Fundamental, the nation's oldest and largest children's literacy organization. She and her husband, Charles S. Robb, a former governor and United States Senator from Virginia, have raised three almost perfect daughters.

Lyndon Baines Johnson was a high school teacher who served his fellow Americans for over thirty years as a member of the United States House of Representatives, Majority Leader of the United States Senate, Vice President, and President of the United States.

Cokie Roberts

■ HALE BOGGS

MY HUSBAND loves to tell the story of asking my father for my hand. Steve was twenty-three years old and nervous as any prospective groom would be about approaching his intended father—his nervousness somewhat exacerbated by the fact that my father, Hale Boggs, was Majority Whip of the House of Representatives at the time, not someone you'd want to take on in a debate. What Steve didn't know was that Daddy was just as nervous. Sensing that something was up (my mother probably gave him a heads-up, as she always did his advance work), he escaped to the garden early in the morning, trying to hide behind the tomato plants. When Steve bravely approached, Daddy handed him a watering can, instructing him to water the tomatoes. Summoning his courage, Steve said that we wanted to get married. It hardly came as a surprise since we had been dating for four years and my father simply shrugged. "Fine." Feeling that something more should be said on this momentous occasion, Steve ploughed on. "I know you think Cokie and I will have problems because of religion (Steve is Jewish, and I am Catholic) but we think we can work them out." Wisely, my father responded, "Yes, I do think you'll have problems, but not half as many problems as I'll have if I try to tell Cokie who to marry."

It's a story that gets at the heart of my relationship with my father. He respected me. He respected my judgment in choosing a husband as he respected my arguments in political debate. I grew up in the 1950s when that was not common, and it made all of the difference in how my life turned out. From the time I was a very little girl (now we're going back to the 1940s) my father always included me and my sister and brother in his political life. It was his and my mother's view that since we suffered all the disadvantages of being political children—particularly in the spicy world of Louisiana politics where no one pulled any punches—we should also enjoy some of the advantages. So we were always invited to join the guests at the dinner table, no matter what their positions. We also got to miss school if there was a particularly important debate on the House floor, or an especially fun campaign event. On Election Day we all went to the polls to greet the voters. Since I was the youngest and couldn't go by myself, Daddy and I paired up. I remember being so proud as he introduced me to his constituents. And we were called on to make speeches from the time we were tiny. Don't get me wrong—these weren't things we had to do. We begged to do them. We loved spending time with our fun-loving father and we loved politics. We knew it mattered, and, if the family wanted us to participate, we must be pretty important too.

As I grew up and talked politics with my father, he always listened to my point of view. He didn't always agree, but he took me seriously. During those years of civil rights struggles my siblings and I constantly pushed him to vote the way he really felt, against all forms of discrimination. Poor guy. Instead of home being the place where he could retreat from the political passions of the day, he faced a whole new round of arguments at the dinner table. But he knew he was the cause of our obstreperousness. He had trained us to take him on. (So, Sam and George, blame Dad.) For years he patiently explained that, as much as he would like to vote for civil rights, he would be defeated for doing it, and the person who beat him would be an ardent segregationist. Then came the Voting Rights Act of 1965, the year after I graduated from college. Steve and I remember so well sitting in the backyard of my parents' house, where we now live, praising Daddy for his decision to vote for the bill the next day but trying to convince him to speak for it as well. "Leave me alone," he grumped, totally exhausted. When debate began in the House and a fellow Louisianan protested that there was no discrimination against African Americans in our home state, my father found he could not hold his tongue. He made one of the most memorable speeches of his career as a Deep Southerner calling on Congress to enforce enfranchisement for blacks. He couldn't wait to tell me what he had done.

Fathers are the first men most girls encounter. How they treat you can shape your relationships with men for the rest of your life. I was blessed. My father treated me always in the best way possible—he treated me as an equal.

■ ■ ■

Cokie Roberts is a political commentator for ABC News *and senior news analyst at* NPR. *She is also the author of three best-selling books and, along with her husband Steven V. Roberts, writes a weekly newspaper column syndicated by United Media.*

Hale Boggs was first elected to Congress from Louisiana in 1940, a few years before Cokie was born. In 1972, Boggs was serving as Majority Leader of the House of Representatives when, while campaigning for a fellow congressman, the plane he was traveling in disappeared over Alaska. The airplane has never been found.

Gracie Rosenberger

■ JIM PARKER

DECEMBER 1983. Never before had I experienced such agony. I swam toward a consciousness that, for the rest of my life, would contain physical pain and suffering.

"I'm here, Gracie. This is Daddy. Daddy's here, Gracie."

Dad was here? I didn't even know where "here" was. The sound of his voice cascaded past the hurt, and I felt his rugged hand on my shoulder and opened my eyes. His face was so big, so close, the tears brimming in his eyes and trickling down his chiseled cheeks.

The last I knew, Dad was 400 miles away and I was testing my wings as a college freshman in Nashville. He slowly filled in the gaps my mind strained to comprehend; how I'd fallen asleep at the wheel, run off the road, crushed both legs and suffered multiple internal injuries. Through the thick fog of pain, I learned my family had rushed up from their home in Florida, only to helplessly watch over me while I lay unconscious for three weeks hovering between life and death.

Following those days, Dad kept vigil at my bedside for more times than I can remember. When I took my first awkward steps on mangled legs, he was there. As he walked me slowly down the aisle to marry Peter, I leaned a little harder on his strong arm. At the birth of both our sons, Dad paced with Peter. When the pain in my legs became more than I could bear and they were amputated, Dad cried with me and held me a little tighter.

The number of operations grew to more than sixty, and I still awoke to see him, often dozing off with his well-thumbed Bible open in his lap, as he agonized over what possible good or purpose could the God he's served so faithfully have in all this suffering. The heartache he's carried over my injuries at times must have felt overpowering to him, yet he remains a constant encouragement in my life.

As I stood in front of the country to sing at the 2004 Republican National Convention, he cheered me on. When I spoke to wounded soldiers at Walter Reed struggling with their own devastating injuries, he wept. But it was when Peter and I went to Africa to bring artificial limbs to destitute amputees that his heartache slowly subsided. When my father saw a man ride into our clinic on his wife's back and walk out with his children dancing around him, Dad was able to look at me and say with confidence, "God 'truly causes all things to work together for good to those that love God, to those who are called according to His purpose.'" *Romans 8:28 (NKJV)*

Raising two daughters, Dad had to learn about dresses, ballet, and even tea parties. To be candid, he wasn't very good at any of those things. But he did give me something of himself that has sustained me through very difficult times: persistence, toughness, and the unswerving belief that God is faithful and we can trust Him with our lives . . . and the lives of our children.

■ ■ ■

Gracie Rosenberger draws on her own journey through more than sixty operations and the amputation of both legs and addresses life's heartaches and disappointments honestly and directly, but full of hope, to audiences across the country. As listeners embrace Gracie's contagious humor, and are drawn into her story of faith and perseverance, they find laughter mixing with their tears as they see that God is working in all things with mercy, love, and purpose. Gracie, along with her husband Peter, founded Standing With Hope, and is the first amputee woman to provide artificial limbs and prosthetic training as an evangelical outreach to developing countries.

Jim Parker retired from a successful career as a land developer in Northwest Florida. Jim, an ordained minister, is known for his deep passion for sharing his faith with hurting individuals. Jim's family helped settle Tennessee in the late 1700s, and has produced numerous national, state, and local political leaders. The Parkers divide their time between Florida and their ranch in Montana.

Wendy Ryan

■ NOLAN RYAN

ONE JANUARY MORNING in 1999, my father, Nolan Ryan, received a telephone call informing him that he had been voted into the National Baseball Hall of Fame in Cooperstown, New York. This is an honor that he and every professional baseball player dream of achieving, and I will always remember being in the family kitchen watching my father's dream come true. It was only fitting that my family and I were there when he got the news because during his entire career, twenty-six years of professional baseball, he always put his family first. It was inspiring to see this wonderful man prove that he did not have to sacrifice one love for another. I remember looking at the bond between my parents, my brothers, and me and thinking that this man should be going into the National Dad Hall of Fame as well.

I am sure that it was not always easy for my father to be a success at home and on the baseball field, but he was an all-star in both places. Baseball, which my brothers and I loved, was a huge part of our lives and our childhoods. We traveled with his team during the summers, played catch on the big league fields before the games, and loved ordering room service in the hotels. He made his job fun for us even though he was working extremely hard. These special memories will stay with me forever, and now, as an adult, I realize that by including us in his job he was keeping the family together. Even when we could not travel with him during school, he was always a part of our daily routines. He called from the ballpark to check our report cards or ask how our volleyball or baseball games went. I always knew that even if he was on a road trip and pitching a big game he was thinking of us at home.

Most everyone knows about the special bond between a father and a daughter, and I am so fortunate to have a wonderful relationship with my dad. It was tough as a little girl watching my brothers get to spend more time with

him than I did because baseball clubhouses and locker rooms are no place for a girl. But as I got older I realized that he, the man that mattered the most, never excluded me from activities because I was a girl. Some of my fondest memories are of us hunting, fishing, hiking, riding horses, playing catch, shooting free throws in the backyard and even playing cards on the airplane. My father taught me that life is not about where you go, what you earn, or what honors you are given. He taught me that life is about the relationships you build with love and the memories you make. Thanks, Dad, for giving me so many wonderful memories and filling my heart with so much love. You are truly a "Hall of Famer" in more ways than one.

■ ■ ■

Wendy Ryan lives in Round Rock, Texas and is currently working with her father on their cattle ranching operation in South Texas.

Nolan Ryan currently lives in Georgetown, Texas and is involved with his ranching operation, is an owner of two minor league baseball teams, and is also employed as a consultant for the Houston Astros.

Sara Shumway

■ NORMAN SHUMWAY

IT SEEMED THAT, while I was growing up, my father enjoyed the simple pleasures of life. This included washing his car in a Speedo so that his varicose veins were displayed nicely. Other times he barbecued steak in the backyard and tormented our dog with fabulous aromas. After such a meal he would say, "Someone's going to make a big hit with the dog." The dog was rewarded with bits of steak table scraps. Later we came to call our dog "The dog" or just "The" for short. A relaxing ski trip by my father's standards was a one-day affair. My brother, sisters, and I rose around 4 a.m., usually on a Wednesday, and were driven to the Tahoe area some five hours away. Skiing lasted from opening, but never quite to closing. The return trip usually got us home by 10 p.m. It was not very restful, but a lot of fun.

My father was a doctor. When I accidentally jumped on a nail in bare feet, he made arrangements for my tetanus shot. About a year later at age eight, I fell off a bicycle and he sewed up my chin using three green stitches. When I was a candy striper, I was goaded into dashing up the down escalator at the hospital. I fell and skinned my knee. He greeted me in the emergency department with, "No stitches, this time."

When I decided to pursue a medical career, he was all for it. His advice was, "Do what you want to do, because then you will get good at it, and it will not seem like work." Occasionally heart surgery does seem like work, but it is work that we have both enjoyed. Recently my first patient to undergo a heart transplant, when I was the attending surgeon, visited my father. It has been over seventeen years since his heart transplant, and he is doing very well. He wanted to show my father that he had derived maximum benefit from a good operation. The patient commented to me via e-mail: "Our visit was short, but long enough to tell that the many good things I had read about his kindness and caring for those around him were not exaggerated."

Last year Dad was diagnosed with a cancer that had already spread to regional lymph nodes. He went through a big operation and several rounds of radiation therapy without a single whine. His goal was to play golf again. He became short of breath just after the New Year and was diagnosed with malignant fluid surrounding both lungs. Any treatment thereafter was just temporizing. He continued to try to have a daily routine, but then opted for hospice care. Dad was grateful for their help and always thanked his care givers. He died just after his 83rd birthday. I will miss his joie de vivre.

■ ■ ■

Sara Shumway is professor of cardiovascular surgery at the University of Minnesota and surgical director of heart transplantation. She trained with surgeons who had trained with her father.

Dr. Norman Shumway was professor of cardiovascular surgery at Stanford University School of Medicine. He was the chief of cardiovascular surgery from 1965 to 1993. He and his friend and colleague Richard Lower did the early experimental work that led to the successful clinical application of heart transplantation in 1967.

Ellen Johnson Sirleaf

■ CARNEY JOHNSON

I WAS TWENTY YEARS OLD when my father died, seven years after he had become paralyzed as a result of a stroke. Medical service in Liberia was way behind in the capacity to diagnose and provide the required rehabilitation following the cerebral vascular accident. I and my three siblings spent the seven years of my father's illness marveling at and assisting a mother who was totally dedicated to his care.

We remembered him with great fondness. He was a handsome and well-dressed figure who attracted a large number of female companions and admirers to the consternation of our mother. His children were proud of him. He was the role model and the idol of his ethnic group (Gola), because of his success in bridging the gap from rural to urban, from "Country" to "Congo," the description given those who originated from the indigenous on the one hand and the settler population on the other. He was born and spent his early years in the village, one of the sons of a powerful chief who sent his best and brightest to reside and be schooled by an urban settler family. This powerful chief, my father's father, was also known as the peacemaker.

Life was hard in his young days as he served his guardian family while trying to get an education. He applied his time, understudied a renowned Liberia lawyer, became a lawyer, married two times to women with similar mixed heritage, and quickly moved up the ladder to become the first indigenous member of the National Legislature. He was one of the confidantes of the longest serving president in Liberia's history. His position took him on many trips abroad to represent Liberia, and his fame grew as one who, despite success, remained with his people, being classified as the "poor man's lawyer". He provided pro bono services for everyone who needed but could not afford a lawyer.

I remember him as one who never forgot his roots. As a result, I and my siblings were required to spend vacation days in the village of his birth where his mother lived. We went with our mother to the village immediately after the closing of school, waiting anxiously for him to join us for the few days that he could spare from his urban activities. His entry to the village invoked a big celebration with the drums and the masked dancers (called devils at that time) in full display. His crossing of the river standing upright in the canoe, sometimes with a gun as he shot birds in the trees above, brought joy and excitement to us as we awaited his arrival on the "farm" across the river. His arrival meant goodies from the city, more sumptuous meals from Mother and grandmother and a walk through the farm to be told the potential of the rubber which was being produced or of cotton which was being experimented. Whenever there, folks, family, and others gathered from the surrounding villages to greet and converse with their famous son.

We loved our father; we were proud of our father. His illness brought the wonderful experiment of life in the village to an end. His success thus forgotten, the inner circle of which he was a part faded away. His children grew up, moving on to marriage and their lives. He died somewhat lonely but with his wife at his side and left behind a memory, a value system, and an ambition that, in me, is finally fulfilled.

■ ■ ■

Ellen Johnson Sirleaf was elected in November of 2005 as Liberia's first female President. Well trained as an accountant and an economist at Madison Business College and at Harvard, Mrs. Johnson Sirleaf, earned her stripes in the Liberian government at several levels including the high post of Finance Minister and in the international arena, in both the private sector and the multinational organizations. Having been im-

prisoned for her political conviction, Ellen Johnson Sirleaf emerged with greater dynamism to seek the high office of President. Failing in the first attempt in 1979, she tried again and succeeded the second time to become Africa's first democratically elected female Head of State.

Carney Johnson was one of many children of Gola Paramount Chief, Jahmale, an indigenous Liberian key mediator between the settlers (Americo-Liberian) and the indigenous people of Liberia. Mr. Johnson went on to become one of the first indigenous persons to be elected to the Liberian House of Representatives. The late Carney Johnson suffered a stroke in 1950 and remained paralyzed until his death in 1958. President Ellen Johnson Sirleaf's pursuit of leadership and justice resonate the life and passion of her father.

Pat Head Summitt

■ RICHARD HEAD

MY DAD was the hardest working man I've known in my lifetime. He gave me the skills and values that carried me from the little girl on the farm to the coach, cutting down the net of the championship-winning Tennessee Lady Vols. I was the fourth of five children—sister to three older brothers. In fact, as I look back, I think that I was more like a fourth son to my father. We grew up on a dairy farm in Clarksville, Tennessee. I can still hear my dad on those early mornings—as we dragged our tired bodies out to the barn—uttering the phrase: "Cows don't take a day off."

You see, that's a lesson we learned at a young age on the farm. Just like the cows couldn't take the day off, we couldn't take the day off either. So we worked after school, before homework and dinner, during the summers, during our free time, didn't take family vacations. I remember all of us watching the ten o'clock weather report each night, planning the next day's tasks. This hard work instilled a natural work ethic in me that has extended to every part of my life. In fact, getting up in the morning and going to work comes more naturally to me than relaxing!

My dad was incredibly supportive of everyone in the family, so supportive that he made sacrifices for us to pursue our dreams. Basketball was, is, my game, and I love to compete. My dad always believed that to be the best you had to play against the best. So he wired the hay loft in the barn so that I could play ball against the boys even at nighttime. Unfortunately, Montgomery County, where we lived, only had a girl's basketball team until the eighth grade. So, when it came time to give up basketball or move, my dad picked up the family, sold the dairy farm, and moved us to Cheatham County, where he opened a grocery store to support us.

Dad continued to be a strong force as the years passed. I tore my ACL during my senior year at UT-Martin. My folks had never seen me play a game

at Martin because they were busy running the family grocery store. That game was the first they had attended. I'll never forget riding in the car with my family to the hospital after the game. The doctor came into the room and informed my dad that there was a decision to be made about having surgery and that I would probably be "ok" without it, would lead a pretty normal life as a housewife. My dad turned to the doctor and said very matter of factly, "She is *going* to play in the *Olympics*." I just looked up at my father, my source of inspiration. My dad put something inside me that night—the idea that *you can never quit; you've got to face the challenge of the rehab* because your dad expects you to make that Olympic team. I felt so much pressure that by the time of the Olympic tryouts I actually shot an airball during the last night of the scrimmages!

Dad not only inspired me as a player, but also as a coach. I remember my first year of coaching. We were playing at Belmont University against a team led by a veteran coach, Betty Wiseman. I had actually been recruited by Belmont in high school, but Dad was adamant that I not live in a big city since I was a "country girl." He was afraid that I would move to Nashville and be corrupted, I guess. So I went to Martin, and it ended up being the best choice for me, as I really grew as a student athlete and later as an international player. I was a little overwhelmed during this first year of coaching and especially at this particular game. We ended up losing by one point. I can still recall that sick feeling in my stomach as my dad walked up to me after the game. He told me, "When you lose by one point, the coach needs to find a way to make up the difference." He wasn't telling me that is was unacceptable to lose but that a coach has to figure out how to be more successful and how to make her players succeed in a close ball game. I cannot describe in words how powerful that message has been in my career.

There are two sides to my coaching. My mother taught me the value of relationships. I am constantly having my student athletes over for dinner and a good home-cooked meal, and I have my mother to thank for teaching me to cook and to form strong relationships with people. My father raised the bar for me as a competitor. He often said, "I see more in you than you see in yourself." He taught me that it was okay to be a female and at the same time to compete and be tough and demanding.

After reading my first book, some people thought that I had a strained relationship with my father. Nothing could have been further from the truth. When I write about his "toughness," I admire it. My dad made me. Much more than bringing me into this world, he created the person that I am today. He saw "something" in me that I see now in the women that I work with every day, and he challenged me so that I can stand here and challenge these women to bring out that "something" in each of them.

■ ■ ■

Pat Head Summitt has been the coach of the University of Tennessee *Lady Vols for the past thirty-two years and in 2005 became the NCAA Career Victory Leader for the most wins in Division I basketball . . . men's or women's.*

Richard Head, in addition to running a dairy farm and a grocery business, was an active member of Mt. Carmel United Methodist Church for over seventy-three years. He served as chairman of the East Montgomery Utility Board for forty years, as a Montgomery County commissioner for six years and was a Cheatham County commissioner for eighteen years. Richard Head passed away on October 23, 2005 after sixty-three years of marriage to Hazel Albright Head. They raised five children together.

Joni Eareckson Tada

■ JOHN K. EARECKSON

NOT LONG AGO my husband Ken was cleaning out our garage when he came through the kitchen door holding up a pair of Canadian crutches. "Do you want to dump these?" he asked. I took one look at the dusty crutches and got a lump in my throat. "They're Daddy's," I quietly said. Ken leaned the crutches against the kitchen wall and went back to his project. The aluminum was scraped and the rubber tips were scuffed, but the crutches brought into focus a flood of memories.

All through his 70s and 80s my father, John Eareckson, hobbled around on crutches because of his arthritis. Daddy had me late in life and, even as a little girl, I used to admire the way he used one of his crutches to shove around chairs or even ring a doorbell. On a good day, I tossed him a ball and he whacked it right past me. Around the farm we could always tell when Dad was off on a horseback ride—his crutches were leaning against the hitching post.

Then came the diving accident in 1967 in which I became paralyzed. Back in the '60s, rehab philosophy hadn't advanced very far and I was forced to stay in the hospital for almost two years. I missed the farm and, oh, I so looked forward to Daddy's visits. I could always tell when he was coming down the hallway to see me. "Click-click," his crutches echoed on the linoleum tile. *Oh boy, Daddy's here!* I grinned, so anxious and happy to see his smile and feel his firm hand on my forehead.

Because of Daddy's arthritis, I believed that he, more than anyone else in the family, understood my situation. I could see it in his eyes and could hear it in his voice when he set down his crutches by my hospital bedside and read to me from his Bible. It's why that "clicking" sound, for me, was such a beautiful, welcoming sound.

My dear father went home to be with Jesus in 1990 at the age of ninety years old and I miss him still. But God brings him to mind every time I read a special Bible verse. Isaiah 52:7 says, "How beautiful on the mountains are the feet of those who bring good news, who proclaim peace, who bring good tidings, who proclaim salvation, who say to Zion, 'Your God reigns!'" No doubt about it. My father's feet may have been disabled with arthritis, but they were beautiful. The sounds of his crutches brought good tidings, peace for my heart, and salvation for my soul.

Oh Lord, my legs may be paralyzed, but I'm reminded of Daddy and the beautiful sound of the way he walked. Make my feet beautiful, Lord . . . may I be mindful to carry the good news of your glad tidings to others today.

■ ■ ■

Joni Eareckson Tada, an author, artist, and founder of Joni and Friends (see www.joniandfriends.org), has been paralyzed for almost forty years as a result of a diving accident.

John K. Eareckson was born in Baltimore in 1900 and during his lifetime he was a Merchant Marine, housing contractor, Boys Brigade leader, champion wrestler, and father of four girls, Joni being the youngest.

Margaret Thatcher

■ ALFRED ROBERTS

I WAS BORN in 1925 in the bustling market town of Grantham, in Lincolnshire, into a very traditional family. My mother, Beatrice, had been a dressmaker with her own business before her marriage, and though she gave that up to work in the family grocers shop she remained a strong and pivotal character. But, as was often the case in those days, my father was very much the centre of the household.

Alfred Roberts came from a family of shoemakers. His ambition had been to become a teacher, but due to family circumstances he had been forced to leave school at thirteen and he eventually settled in the grocery trade. At the outbreak of the First World War he tried to enlist in the army, indeed over the course of the war he tried to enlist six times, but on each occasion he was turned down on medical grounds. His brother, who did join the army, was killed in action in 1917. These early events in his life strongly shaped his character and years later, through his influence, would shape mine.

My father's shortened school life spurred him towards educating himself. He had a passion for reading and self-improvement which as a young girl I soon began to follow. Each week he would take me to the local library where I chose two books. One would be a work of fiction—poetry or literature— while the second would be more serious—a history or biography. Both books had to be read during the week and before they were returned my father would discuss each with me to ascertain my opinions and to see what I had learned. This practice, from an early age, not only made me a very quick reader but also gave me a strong memory, both of which were to be of great benefit in my political career. My father was determined that I should have what he dearly would have liked himself, the best possible education—an education which would take me first to the local grammar school and then on to Oxford.

My father's frustration at not being able to serve in the army, and the loss of his brother, strengthened further his great sense of patriotism and his belief in doing one's duty for the country. In the 1930s I often sat and listened as he and his friends discussed the latest international issues, particularly developments in Germany, and he encouraged me to write to my penfriend, a young Jewish girl living in Austria, who a few years later we helped by bringing her to Grantham. He was most distrustful of all the talk of disarmament and alarmed that Britain might not be prepared if the worst came to pass. His conviction that we should never give in to bullies and that we must remain strong greatly influenced my approach much later towards the Soviet Union and communism.

Duty was important to him in another way. He believed that he had a duty to his customers who came to our shop. He believed he had a duty towards the local community: he was actively involved with charity and on the local town council, ultimately becoming mayor. And he believed that politics should be about civic duty too. So when I embarked upon my political career, I was instilled with a sense that politics was not just about personal ambition, climbing ever higher up the "greasy pole." Politics was only worthwhile if you were doing what was right to better your country and to benefit its people. As we listened to the radio, hearing the latest reports of terror from Germany or the Soviet Union, he shook his head in despair at the oppression that men, through the mechanisms of the State, could inflict upon one another. For him, the capacity of the State to do harm regularly outweighed its potential to do good. The more freedom individuals enjoyed, the more choices and decisions they could make for themselves, then the better life would be—a political philosophy I readily took up.

Given my father's fascination and passion for politics, it should really have been no surprise that I should take up the family mantle—but as a woman in the 1950s my chosen career path did surprise many. Discussions on current affairs, local, national, and international, were a constant feature in our household. The hardships of the 1930s gave way to the horrors of war, and the huge economic and social changes which came afterwards. Though only children, my father believed that my sister, Muriel, and I should be aware of what was happening in the world and he encouraged us to hold views about it. We were always included with the adults, perhaps spared only on a few rare occasions when the full horror of man's evil towards his fellow man was thought too gruesome for our ears. A decade or so later it was sometimes felt rather ahead of its time that any young woman should have developed strong and fixed opinions, but for me it was a natural result of my father's approach.

If family, the shop, and his civic obligations were the first three pillars of my father's life, then the Methodist Church was the fourth. He was an active member of our local chapel and much in demand in the area as a lay preacher. From him I was infused with a belief that there is a moral code which should guide us all: that right and wrong should be recognised, not blurred; and that God created us all as unique individuals. He believed that we all had a responsibility towards ourselves, our family, and the wider community. If you did not work hard to provide for yourself and those around you, how could you care for others truly in need? His unshakeable Christian faith gave him, and subsequently me, a firm and fixed set of values—what I came to call a moral compass. Through our actions we could make a difference, for good or ill. As a favourite verse of mine by Ella Wheeler Wilcox went,

> One ship drives East, and another drives West,
> By the self-same gale that blows;
> 'Tis the set of the sail, and not the gale,
> That determines the way she goes.

During childhood it is difficult fully to realise how much our parents and their teachings affect our own characters, but looking back it becomes much more clear. My father was my example. He inspired me in my beliefs and my ambitions. He guided me, encouraged me, and spurred me forward. He did not live to see me become a Cabinet Minister and then Prime Minister, but I like to think that he would be very pleased with the result.

■ ■ ■

Margaret Thatcher was born in 1925, at Grantham in Lincolnshire. She and her elder sister Muriel were brought up in the flat above their parents' grocery shop. She studied chemistry at Oxford University and became a research chemist with a large company before qualifying as a lawyer. She married Denis in 1951 and gave birth to twins two years later. Always interested in politics, she entered Parliament in 1959 as MP for

Finchley. She quickly rose through various ministerial jobs, eventually becoming Secretary of State for Education and Science. After two successive Conservative defeats in the general elections in 1974, she replaced Edward Heath as leader and in 1979 took the Conservatives back into power. She served as Britain's first female Prime Minister for eleven and a half years and won two further general elections, making her the longest serving British Prime Minister of the twentieth century.

Alfred Roberts came from a Northamptonshire family and settled in Grantham in 1913. He established himself in the grocery trade and four years later he married a local dressmaker, Beatrice Stephenson. They had two daughters: Muriel and Margaret. Alfred was active in his local community as a strong Methodist and lay preacher, a keen Rotarian, and served for many years on the local town council, ultimately becoming mayor. He died in 1970.

Shirley M. Tilghman

■ HENRY W. CALDWELL

A **GLORIOUS THING** about my father is that he never thought of me as "a girl." This freed me to create for myself an identity that was not constrained by the prevailing stereotypes of the 1950s about women's roles in society. The father of four daughters, he probably would have liked a son, although he denied this vehemently to his daughters. Instead he treated his daughters as he would have treated his sons, encouraging each of us to think of the world as our oyster, its opportunities infinite and limited only by our talents, interests, and ambition.

He was always my fierce champion. In high school I loved chemistry and mathematics and was certain that I wanted to become a scientist, something my father supported without reservation. As someone who came of age during the Great Depression he was adamant that his children have careers and be self-supporting. When a guidance counselor suggested that I should abandon any thoughts about science, which after all, is not "meant for girls," and redirect my talents to a profession for which I was more suited—her recommendation was to become an executive secretary—my father was first incredulous, and then furious. Without the benefit of having read Betty Friedan's *The Feminine Mystique*, which was published that same year, my father laid down the feminist gauntlet to the principal at Kelvin High School. No one was going to tell his daughter not to follow her dream.

Years later, shortly after I was married, my husband and I were applying to law school and graduate school simultaneously. My mother-in-law was scandalized that I was not taking the usual path of working to support my husband through law school, and she called my father to solicit his help in persuading me to forgo my education. The seeds of her proposal fell on unsympathetic soil, to say the least. I have come to appreciate that my father's unswerving faith in my ability to accomplish whatever I set my mind and heart to was the rock on which I have built my life.

The impact that a supportive father can have on a young woman's confidence in venturing outside societal norms is profound. In the 1990s I attended a meeting of women leaders in science and engineering at Mills College in Oakland, California. Before the meeting each participant filled out a questionnaire about her life, and the circumstances that led her to a career in science. Remarkably the one characteristic that this group of academic, government, and private sector leaders had in common was supportive parents. Some of us had had exceptional teachers along the way; some had not. Some had had professional mentors who had paved the way for them; some had not. Some had supportive husbands and partners; some had not. But the vast majority of the very successful women at this meeting reported that, from a young age, their parents had not limited their horizons by suggesting that some professions were more appropriate than others for girls. Like my mother and father, their parents had given them permission to dream.

■ ■ ■

Shirley M. Tilghman is a professor of molecular biology and the nineteenth president of Princeton University.

Henry W. Caldwell was an executive of the Bank of Nova Scotia by day, and a golfer and jazz pianist at all other times.

Pam Tillis

■ MEL TILLIS

THE WESTERN SWING GIANT Bob Wills recorded a song, "Time Changes Everything," that my dad loves to perform. Coincidentally, that title summarizes perfectly the history of our father-daughter bond. In fact, country music fans that know a little bit about me and my dad know we have had our share of problems. However, our problems were surely shaped by the difficult environment we lived in—the music business, a path we would ironically share later in life.

Back to the beginning . . . we came to Nashville just before my first birthday. During my formative years, Dad was a man on fire for his craft. He had discovered he could write hit songs, and uttered lines from them over and over. Often, I'd wake up in the middle of the night, hearing him singing his latest song to my mom. My dreams were literally filled with music. As a teenager I was this skinny, shy, and self-conscious girl, and, because of my dad's busy "hillbilly singing" career, I felt even more of a misfit. He was "on the road" all the time, and when he came home there was always an awkward period of readjustment even though we longed to be closer. It also seemed like he was tougher on me in many ways because I was the oldest and his expectations were high. He often called me "Olive Oyl" (after the cartoon character), trying to teach me to laugh at myself. He had learned that lesson many years earlier from the great Minnie Pearl, who had encouraged him to do the same. Though I didn't see it at the time, he was teaching me to let things roll off my back, an invaluable lesson in a business where we are constantly judged.

Somewhere along that time line, I caught the music fever too. This gift of music was his legacy to me, among other talents, and it is something I am so grateful for. In fact, this gratitude propelled me to go back in his archives in 2001 and listen to every song my dad had written. Some were obscure and

hard to find, but in a giant "labor of love" I recorded thirteen of my favorite Mel Tillis songs as a way of saying thanks to that "hillbilly singer."

I've learned a lot on my own as well, teaching myself to play the guitar and sing. Dad said, "Somewhere along the line you went from being a good singer to a great singer." That meant a lot coming from a man who doesn't hand out fake compliments. I'm so glad I earned his respect. I also learned to have a sense of pride from my father. A job worth doing is a job worth doing right. I also came to learn over the lonely miles I've spent on my own tour bus how much Daddy must have missed us, and how he couldn't help not always being there. He had his share of regrets too, and I learned big dreams have big price tags as well. Time changes everything, and these days Dad gives more hugs and is freer with his "I love you's," an example I try to follow with my son.

As kids, we used to love to shine Daddy's show boots. He had a wooden shoeshine box complete with black Cordova polish and a boar bristle brush. So we went to work on his boots when he returned from the road. We didn't see it as a chore because he taught us a job well done is its own satisfaction. Now, as I have matured, it means so much to see how happy it makes people whenever we perform together. I am lucky to still have him and I cherish every minute we have. Now I'm the one that laughs when he calls me Olive Oyl because I realize that, although I no longer resemble that skinny little knock-kneed kid, Daddy will always see me as that little girl.

■ ■ ■

Recording artist and songwriter *Pam Tillis* has sold over six million records, received two Grammy awards, three CMA awards, including Female Vocalist of the Year, and seven ACM nominations. Of Pam's sixteen Top Ten hits, seven went straight to #1 on the Billboard charts.

Mel Tillis penned his first hit, "I'm Tired" recorded by Webb Pierce, in 1956. A member of the Songwriter Hall of Fame, Mel has written over 1000 songs including "Ruby," "Detroit City," and "I Ain't Never." He was the CMA's Comedian of the Year for six straight years and was awarded the CMA's Entertainer of the Year in 1976.

Kathleen Kennedy Townsend

■ ROBERT F. KENNEDY

MY FATHER MADE LIFE a great adventure. One major part of that adventure was sports. He loved to wear his sweater with the "H" that he had earned for playing varsity football at Harvard. For him, athletics was a big part of keeping fit—physically and mentally. Each weekend we took long walks around McLean, Virginia—in the woods, along the streams. (This was before sprawl transformed McLean from farm country to upscale suburb.) Sports gave us the opportunity to test ourselves against our own best efforts as well as other competitors. My father loved to ride, to ski, to sail, to hike, to play capture the flag and, of course, touch football.

He admired athletic achievement. Our home was always filled with my father's friends who were renowned for great feats: Jim Whittaker, the first American up Everest; Rafer Johnson, an Olympic decathlon athlete; Tommy Corcoran, an Olympic downhill racer on the American ski team; Willie Schaeffer, a great skier and coach; Rosey Grier, a football star; and John Glenn. His best friend was a renowned high school athlete, Dave Hackett, who John Knowles used as the prototype for the adolescent hero Phineas in *A Separate Peace*.

That same sense of striving for excellence and willingness to take on all comers shaped his public life. My father was deeply committed to justice. He attacked corruption in the teamsters even though labor unions were seen as critical to his brother's presidential campaign; as Attorney General he challenged J. Edgar Hoover to acknowledge the existence of organized crime despite the power of Hoover and organized crime; and he took on segregationist Southerners despite the fact that it would hurt his brother in the next election.

And, he wanted my brothers and sisters to know and understand the im-

portance of all of this. Yes, we too rode and skied and tried to catch the long throw. But more important, I learned from my father to love justice. When other three- and four-year-olds were taken to the playground, I went to the Senate Rackets Committee Hearings. He took us to the Justice Department and described the terrible ways in which discrimination forced Americans to live in poverty, both material and spiritual.

When we flew to New York, he made sure we went through Harlem. He wanted us to understand that many families did not have a place for the children to play—no swings, no sandbox. Hardly a tree. He launched a restoration effort in Bedford-Stuyvesant because he knew it's not enough to complain; one must solve problems.

When his brother died, he showed us how to live. Despite his terrible sadness and sense of loss, he knew that he had a role to play, that he could not give up. He had a strong sense of responsibility.

One spring evening I particularly remember. He had just returned from hunger hearings in Mississippi. We were about to sit down for Sunday dinner. The table was set, the linen tablecloth, the china, and silverware all beautifully placed. And he walked in. He described how he had been to a shack where a whole family lived in a place the size of our dining room and how the children had distended stomachs because they had not enough to eat, and how one child was covered with sores because there was no health care. "Do you know how lucky you are?" he asked. "Do you know how lucky you are? You have a special responsibility to our country."

He was right. He taught me so much by his example. Now, hardly a day passes that someone does not tell me how much my father meant to him, how he helped, how he inspired. I am very lucky.

■ ■ ■

Kathleen Kennedy Townsend has a long history of accomplishment in the public arena. She served as Maryland's first woman Lieutenant Governor and Deputy Assistant Attorney General of the United States. She is an avid reader and mother of four daughters.

Robert F. Kennedy served as a United States Senator and as the Attorney General of the United States. Throughout his life and his time as a public servant he tackled the toughest problems facing our society with enormous strength and boldness.

■ BEN VEREEN

WHEN I WAS a little girl I stood in the wings of majestic theaters watching my father light up the stage. His smile was and still is contagious. I watched him fly across the stage and then peep around the curtain to see the hundreds of faces in awe of him. And so was I and continue to be as I see him define the word legend.

My father grew up in Bedford Stuyvesant Brooklyn, a menacing neighborhood coined "Bed Stye Do or Die." He resided on Herkimer, which for many was a one-way street to the next block, but for my father it led straight to Broadway. Life handed him two options: a knife or a pair of dance shoes. Thank God for us he chose the shoes and in doing so lifted the Vereen family name out of the streets to marquees and ultimately into the history books. My father's talent has been rewarded with honors, and his charity work with the disabled and aspiring young entertainers has transformed many lives.

It wasn't an easy road for my dad; he had obstacles named racism, addiction, tragedy, and paralysis, all of which he overcame. But watching my father learn to live again was the most inspiring story of them all. My father became a superhero after he was struck by a pick-up truck on Pacific Coast Highway in Malibu. He was so critically injured that my mother decided to send for my sister and me. So we anxiously waited, but I couldn't escape it. It was in sympathetic glances and scrolled on the bottom of the after-school specials. Being a celeb kid is hard when a family tragedy becomes the latest on the six o'clock news. I learned myths about my father's condition from the television. "He's talking, alert. It's just a broken leg." It was all wrong, but even I was disillusioned by the media. Nothing could prepare me for what I was about to see when my mother sent for my sister, Kabara, and I.

We arrived at UCLA hospital and were greeted by our mother, who is the epitome of strength. She carried us through our sister Naja's death just a few years earlier, and in true Kentucky Bruner fashion she became our Gibraltar once again. We approached the cold, steel door of the ICU unit. She calmly instructed us not to be afraid and to ignore what we were about to see. "Focus on his eyes. There," she said, " you will find your father."

I walked into the ICU and was shocked; all my illusions of my father's minor injuries were destroyed. It was worse than I could have ever imagined. My father was unrecognizable. He was hooked up to so many machines and computers. He was swollen, his head was shaved and adorned with a crown of monitors, his leg was broken and suspended in the air by metal rods, his stomach was split wide open and a traecheotomy had been performed on his golden throat. It was horrific. I slowly walked to his bedside and he opened his eyes. My mother was right; there he was and happy to see me. I grabbed his hand, and the monitors beeped of joy. He attempted to speak but the traecheotomy tube arrested his voice. His lips read, " I love you."

My family camped outside the ICU unit for weeks. He endured many surgeries and many bad days. The doctors delivered us news of paralysis on his right side. His chances of singing and dancing were unlikely. Rehabilitation on his body would soon follow. It consisted of him just sitting up in the bed on his own. It would be a long road to an unknown recovery.

My father's faith and strength soon dumbfounded the hospital as he quickly proved them all wrong. Every day was a struggle, a fight for his life that he fought with fierce determination. Soon his traecheotomy tube was removed; he covered the hole in his throat to sing. We were relieved to hear his silky voice emerge. Soon he raced through the hospital hallways in a wheelchair and soon my mother and I rolled him out the hospital doors. He felt the morning air on his face, and his smile beamed brighter than the sun. There in his face I saw rebirth, resurrection, faith, and there at that moment my father taught me anything is possible. Six months later, after the doctors said he would never walk again, he gracefully stepped onstage in Broadway's *Jelly's Last Jam*. That night we all witnessed Ben Vereen, a miracle walking, a miracle dancing, a miracle singing. God is good.

■ ■ ■

Ka-ron Om Vereen, the youngest of five children of Ben Vereen, is a filmmaker working in Los Angeles, California. She is currently working on a documentary on the Black Cowboys of Compton. Inspired by her father's struggle in Hollywood as an African American actor, she strives to create positive roles for African American talent.

Ben Vereen is a legendary triple threat who has received many awards for his talents and community service. He made his mark on Broadway in shows such as Jesus Christ Super Star, Jelly's Last Jam, Hair, *and* Grind. *He won the prestigious Tony Award and Drama Desk Award for his outstanding performance in* Pippin. *He won the hearts of America as* Chicken George *in the Emmy-winning series* Roots. *He has appeared in several television shows and theater productions. He travels the country as a motivational speaker and reverend, tackling issues such as overcoming adversity, the arts and education, and black history. He is currently on Broadway in* Wicked *and can be seen in Outkast's musical* Idlewild.

Jessica Waltrip
Sarah Kaitlyn Waltrip

■ DARRELL WALTRIP

JESSICA WALTRIP

MY DAD WORKS in the broadcast booth for FOX Sports six months out of the year, from January to the end of June. He does work the other six months out of the year, but not nearly as much. When he first starts back working in January after being home with us for several months, it always seems very odd and slightly lonely when he is suddenly gone for days and sometimes weeks at a time. He doesn't like being apart from us either, but he is ALWAYS ready to get back to his beloved sport after so many months of not being around it. Although my daddy is sad to leave us, the anticipation of hearing the "beautiful" sounds of race cars going around in circles at 200 miles per hour is enough to make the leaving part somewhat better for him.

Daytona is the first race of the season. In 2004, Dad left for Daytona and was gone for two weeks right off the bat. This stretch of time included being gone for his birthday and also Valentine's Day. In our family, Valentine's Day is always a big deal. We make it a really special day by going out to eat and buying each other cards and chocolate. Dad always gives my mom a dozen red roses, and he also gets both me and my sister half a dozen roses each! I was sad that my dad could not be with us that Valentine's Day. To make sure Dad knew we loved and missed him, we decided to make him a special gift. We made a CD with some of his favorite songs. We baked him a batch of cookies and also included our Valentine's cards. We sent the gift off, hoping it would brighten his Valentine's Day.

My mom, sister, and I received our roses the morning of Valentine's Day. My dad called us that morning to thank us for our thoughtful gift. He told us

he loved us and apologized for not being with us on that day. He also assured us that he would make it up to us when he got home. Even though I was happy about my flowers, I was also a little sad that they could not be given to us in person by my daddy.

We went on with our day, without my dad, by helping my sister get ready for two performances that she was in that day. Even though we had a lot going on, my dad leaves a big hole in our hearts when he is on the road. We missed him. My sister's first performance was over in the middle of the afternoon, so we had a little downtime before the second performance began. Right as the first performance ended, my mom began telling my sister and me that we needed to hurry home right away. My sister and I couldn't understand what the rush was because my sister had three hours before we needed to be ready for the next performance. Mom kept insisting that we get home as soon as possible to check on the dogs because one was ailing at the time. We all hurried to the car and drove home. When we got into the house my mom told me to go upstairs and help my sister while she went to see about our border collie. Just as my sister and I were headed up the stairs, my mom started yelling, "JESSICA! SARAH KAITLYN! COME LOOK AT THIS!" We rushed into where my mom was standing and my dad walked out from behind the door! We couldn't believe our eyes! It was a complete shock. He was supposed to be in Daytona Beach and here he was with us. My sister and I ran up to Dad and hugged him with delight. It was a very happy moment.

We couldn't believe that Dad had come home early to celebrate Valentine's Day with us and to see my sister perform as the witch in Hansel and Gretel. My family sat around the table that night eating supper together, laughing, and talking. We were deeply touched when Dad told us he had given up the opportunity to escort President Bush around the racetrack before the Daytona 500. I know that was hard for my dad to give up because he admires and respects President Bush so very much. He came home because he and my mom had already made plans for him to surprise us the day that the president arrived at the race track. He told President Bush that he would be unable to escort him to the race that day because he needed to get home to be with his family on Valentine's Day. As I watched Dad's face that night, it was so apparent how much he loved us. There was no bitterness about having to give up anything to come home, only an expression of joy that he got to be with his three valentines.

My dad, in spite of being the busy man that he is, is always there when we need him. He takes the time to take us places when he really could be at home working on something far more important than driving me to play practice or something like that. But he always seems to manage things like that with a smile on his face.

One Sunday, we were sitting in church and our pastor announced that the next Saturday night there would be a father-daughter dance. My dad asked me to go to the dance with him! Of course, I accepted. Now my dad may be a talker on TV, but he is NO dancer! My dad, when he is in town, likes to be at home. He is the kind of person who is a homebody!

I needed an outfit to wear so that I would look nice for the dance and for my daddy. My dad, who doesn't like shopping, took my mom and me shopping for a good "dancin'" outfit.

The next Saturday night I was ready to dance! As I walked down the stairs, I think that my dad got tears in his eyes! He looked like the perfect Prince Charming to me—all dressed in a dark suit and tie. I must have looked like Cinderella to him! He said that he couldn't believe how grown up his little girl was. We got into the car and headed to the dance. When we got to the dance, there was a photographer there and my dad insisted that we get our picture taken together. We went in and got refreshments and sat down. There were a few other dads at the dance that my dad knew and that made him feel a little more comfortable about the situation that he found himself in. Soon into the night, we found out that there were two instructors there to teach us a few dance moves. It's a good thing they were there! Otherwise I would have been so embarrassed about how my dad danced I probably wouldn't have shown my face ever again! We did ballroom dancing, the rumba, and even swing dancing. All of this from a father who doesn't like to dance! Our last dance was the Electric Slide. Watching my dad dance the Electric Slide was probably the funniest thing I have ever seen in my whole life. He was about three beats off, didn't know it, and, if he had known, he wouldn't have cared, but he was still having fun! After the dance we went to SONIC and got ice cream. What a date!

I really felt loved when my dad took the time, and got totally out of his comfort box, to take me to the dance. The only time I have ever seen my dad dance was in the kitchen with my mom and it wasn't very pretty! For that night I, no matter how silly this might sound, felt like Cinderella. With the music and the swishing of the skirts and beautiful dresses, it took me back in time and again I felt like I was four, dancing with my dad in my "ball gown" (which was really my nightgown). My daddy holding my hand and dancing with me made me feel really loved and special.

■ ■ ■

Jessica Waltrip, eighteen, is a home-schooled senior in high school.

Sarah Kaitlyn Waltrip, thirteen, is a home-schooled seventh grader.

Nextel Cup Champion Darrell Waltrip is currently a FOX Sports analyst for the Nextel Cup Series.

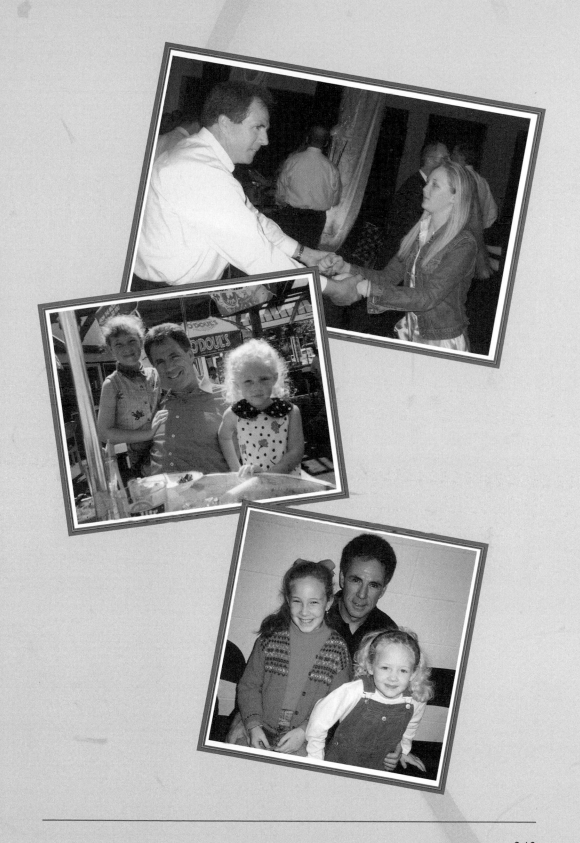

KIMBERLY WILLIAMS-PAISLEY

■ GURNEY WILLIAMS III

I N AN E-MAIL MESSAGE, my dad once described the way he feels about his family. "Known you all for eternity," he wrote. "See you fresh every time we meet. Wonder who you'll be tomorrow."

Tomorrow came late today in Los Angeles because my alarm didn't go off. My phone woke me up at 5:28 a.m. A crabby woman on the other end of the line in New York City told me it was time to do my first live telephone interview of the morning. Fourteen other bouts with drive-time radio hosts followed over the next two hours to publicize an episode of my show, *According to Jim*, that I had directed for the first time in my life.

"We're going live to Orlando in one minute," Crabby said. In my dream-state, I thought I heard "Atlanta."

Less than sixty seconds later, I tried to mute-button the frogs croaking just below the surface of my voice by talking louder. Toward the end of the interview, I threw in a plug for the city that's always been on my top-ten list. "I love Atlanta!" I said.

"Okay," the host said with somewhat less enthusiasm than I'd expected. End of interview. Crabby came on again and said, "That was Orlando. You've got ten minutes before the next call." She hung up. I picked up the phone right away and speed-dialed my dad at home.

He answered, as he always does, within the first two rings. He was in New York, in the same time zone as Crabby, and I knew he'd be awake.

"Hello, this is Gurney Williams," he said. Dad has worked at home as a journalist for the last twenty years, and I'm used to his answering the phone this way. The sound of his voice made me feel better instantly. He is the "command center" of our family—the first one we call with a problem or question.

He is the one who is most curious about our stories. And he is the one who knows how to catch us when we're falling down.

"Guess what I just did," I said. I told him about my mix-up, and he laughed and groaned with me and, then, to make me feel better, shared some of his less-than-great media moments.

Once, when he was a guest on Oprah Winfrey's early-morning live TV show in Baltimore long before she was the great icon she is today, he accidentally called her "Okra." He knew right away he was off her list even before she had a list. On another talk-TV show about the future, most panelists shouted at each other. Dad talked quietly about Sigmund Freud's theories about love and work. During a commercial break, a producer told the panelists, "Most of you are doing great, but you"—looking at Dad—"you need to make more noise."

"I'm really grateful to talk to you," he said, as we were hanging up. Leave it to Dad. I felt back on track after our conversation, ready to face Crabby and the other fourteen cities. He'd given me a much-appreciated gift, once again, in his love, in his listening to my silly story, in his understanding how I felt without having to tell him much. And, as he has done my whole life, Dad also made me feel like I was the one giving him the gift.

I remember another e-mail he once sent: "O firstborn, you move and animate me, and sometimes hold up a mirror to my face."

You too, Daddy.

■ ■ ■

Kimberly Williams-Paisley is an actor, writer, and director. In two of her films—Father of the Bride *and* Father of the Bride Part II—*she brought to the screen the classic father–daughter relationship. She lives with her husband, country singer Brad Paisley, in Los Angeles, California, and Nashville, Tennessee. She's been a fan of her dad her whole life.*

Gurney Williams III *began his journalistic career at* Newsday, *has written for many national magazines, and was the editor of* OMNI *in the mid-1980s. He enjoys working with teenagers at his church and having long dinners whenever possible with his wife Linda and their three grown children.*

Katie Wright

■ BOB WRIGHT

MY DAD is a brilliant guy. But he would be the first to say his achievements in life are the result of hard work rather than just intelligence. From my first years in school, he tried to teach me the importance of hard work and education. Unfortunately, I was a slow learner.

To my dad's endless frustration, I rushed through my homework as quickly as possible in order to give my full attention to *General Hospital* and phone calls to my friends. Dad complained that my geometry grades were awful. I complained that geometry was pointless. He told me that life was not fair. And he pointed out that I would encounter many challenges in life in which I would have to work hard for skills that did not come easily, but that I could do it. I wish I could say I listened. But I most likely mumbled something and turned my attention back to *Family Ties*.

Fortunately, I grew up. By the time I got to college I had learned to appreciate the satisfaction of learning new things and mastering new skills. In fact, I couldn't stop. My poor Dad had created a monster. Eight years and three degrees later my parents were thousands of dollars poorer, but I knew how lucky I was. I was grateful for my education, which expanded my horizons and opened so many doors for me. Little did I know that the biggest challenges still lay ahead and that I would have to work harder than I ever dreamed possible.

Two years ago my oldest son was diagnosed with autism. To say it was devastating would be an understatement. My beautiful, sweet two-year-old, who was full of smiles, giggles, and chatter about Barney and his "Mor Mor" (Grandma), suddenly stopped speaking, playing, laughing, using the potty, everything. Autism is horrible on so many levels. But the lack of knowledge in the medical community and the near absence of government attention to an epidemic affecting nearly 1.5 million people in this country alone are unbelievable.

Everyone told us to accept it, to move on, that Christian will never get any better, and that no one will ever find a cause or a cure. But Dad had taught me the difference between life not being fair and being a fatalist. Together with my mom, he founded Autism Speaks, an organization dedicated to funding research and raising awareness about autism, and ultimately helping children like my Christian, who have been stolen from us by this mysterious neurological disorder.

We are not walking away from this because it is hard. My son and every child in the world with autism deserves better. I have read a hundred books on the subject. I have had to teach myself all there is to know in order to understand my child and find him the best treatment. Most doctors simply do not know what to do. Often they offer genetics as an explanation. My dad and I are no scientists, but we do know there is no such thing as a genetic epidemic, and we do not believe the dramatic increase in incidence rates from 1 in 10,000 twelve years ago to 1 in 166 today is the result of better diagnoses.

My dad is enormously brave to take on autism. It's a controversial and frightening disorder that's been hidden in society's closet for far too long. But I have spent years watching him take on challenge after challenge, with everyone telling him "don't try" or "it will never work," only to see him plow ahead and succeed. He did that in building NBC from a traditional network broadcaster to a diversified multimedia powerhouse called NBC Universal. And he will do it with the fight against autism.

Because of my dad I am relentless in the search for answers and I have found the courage to talk about what I believe is happening. He's been there for me and my family every step of the way, with research, emotional support, financial assistance, logistical help—whatever we need. We are in this together and we are not giving up.

■   ■   ■

Katie Wright graduated from Boston University in 1991 with a B.A. in history. After a year of graduate studies at Cambridge University in the United Kingdom, Katie attended Columbia University Teacher's College where she earned masters degrees in education and psychology. After completing her education, Katie became a licensed therapist. For several years, Katie was the clinical director of the Sexual Assault Crisis Center in Stamford, Connecticut. Katie currently resides in New York City with her husband and two sons, Christian, 4, and Mattias, 2.

Bob Wright is vice chairman and executive officer of General Electric and chairman and chief executive officer of NBC Universal. Bob has had one of the longest and most successful tenures of any media company chief executive. Along with his wife, Suzanne, Bob serves as co-founder of Autism Speaks, a new initiative dedicated to raising public awareness and research funds for autism. Bob is a graduate of the College of the Holy Cross and the University of Virginia School of Law. He and Suzanne have three grown children and four grandchildren.

■ ACKNOWLEDGMENTS

THERE WERE MANY PEOPLE that helped make this dream become a reality. I would first like to thank my husband, Bill and our 3 sons, Harrison, Jonathan and Bryan. They encouraged me, suggested names, proof read stories and NEVER told me to stop talking about the book, even though I am sure they were getting weary of discussing it. They all had important things going on in their lives, such as where to go to college, getting Supreme Court Justices approved, Senior thesis in college and and starting college, but their unfailing support of this book kept me charging forward with my dream .

My sister, Trisha Thomas helped me remember things about Daddy. She even found the perfect photo for the front of the book. We talked often about memories we had of him. She has always supported everything I have done. She is an unselfish loving sister, who I always looked up to and admire to this day.

Dozens of people helped me during the last 3-4 years, but the person without whom I could not have finished the book is my assistant, Mary Ann Voigt. Her enthusiasm and persistence kept me on track. The sad part for both of us, was that her father, Anthony Voigt, died in the fall before we finished the book. Perhaps this sad event is the one thing that gave us determination to complete this project and honor fathers.

Many people suggested names to me, and of course the number one name people mentioned was Oprah. Everyone would say, " You HAVE to have Oprah!"

Well, I do not have Oprah but I do have many fabulous women. Hours were spent trying to get past protective assistants and often only by finding the right person was I able to make the request. Several names come to mind that helped open doors for me; Fred Ryan, Julie Frist, Corinne Barfield, Andrea Newman, Woo Caroland, and Liz Tirrell. Others who helped were Rae Evans, Elizabeth Galvin, Ray Benton, Lucy Calutti, Kitty Moon, Bill McDermott, Ann Furrow, and Jean Ann Banker to name a few. Without these people's help I would never been able to complete the book.

One of my main support groups was the FOK, a group of friends that are always there for me. They gave me many suggestions and comments. One day when I was discouraged and emailed them and said, "Why did I start this project?!" One of them emailed back and said, "Because you loved your dad," and she was correct.

Will Fulgueras was the person who helped me with the photos. The book would not be complete without the photos. Many of them were extremely old and he always was able to get the photo to reproduce.

The final person I would like to thank is Jed Lyons. I remember 4 years ago when he came to our house early in the morning to hear my idea about a book. He and Bill sat and listened to me ramble about my father, how I wanted to honor him and his life, as well as other fathers in a book. I jumped from the chapel I did, to gardening, to photos, etc. Both Jed and Bill looked at me, nodding their heads and said nothing. A year later I met with Jed again. I was thrilled, I had 5 stories. He looked at me and said he wanted around 70 stories . . . I only had 65 to go! He never gave up on me, although I wonder if he questioned if I would ever complete the book!

■ ABOUT THE AUTHOR

KARYN MCLAUGHLIN FRIST was born in Lubbock, Texas, where she grew up with her parents and one sister. After earning a bachelor's degree in teaching from Texas Christian University, she taught physically and mentally disabled children in the local public schools in Dallas, Texas. She is an advocate for the arts and women's and children's health issues. Karyn is also a private pilot and in her free time enjoys gardening and physical fitness. She and her husband, U.S. Senate Majority Leader Bill Frist, live with their three sons—Harrison, Jonathan, and Bryan—in Nashville, Tennessee, and Washington, DC

My Dad

■ _____

_____
_____
_____
_____
_____
_____
_____
_____
_____
_____
_____
_____
_____
_____
_____